WALL STREET SMARTS

WALL STREET SMARTS

A Guide to Finding Your Inner Investor

Miles Goodwin

For information, address Loughlin Investment Group, LLC at wallstreetsmarts.books@gmail.com

ISBN-13: 9781517413927
ISBN-10: 1517413923
Library of Congress Control Number: 2015915642
CreateSpace Independent Publishing Platform
North Charleston, South Carolina

This book does not provide investment advice. Before making any investment, you should either consult with your financial advisor or conduct your own thorough research. Even then you may incur losses, since there is no surefire way to succeed on Wall Street.

"It is the good life," Le Cagot said lazily. "I have traveled, and I have turned the world over in my hand, like a stone with attractive veining, and this I have discovered: a man is happiest when there is a balance between his needs and his possessions. Now the question is: how to achieve this balance. One could seek to do this by increasing his goods to the level of his appetites, but that would be stupid. It would involve doing unnatural things—bargaining, haggling, scrimping, working. *Ergo?* Ergo, the wise man achieves the balance by reducing his needs to the level of his possessions. And this is best done by learning to value the free things of life: the mountains, laughter, poetry, wine offered by a friend, older and fatter women. Now me? I am perfectly capable of being happy with what I have. The problem is getting enough of it in the first place!"

—Beñat Le Cagot, *Shibumi*, Trevanian[1]

To my children: Kate, Daniel, and Susan.
This was written to you and for you.

CONTENTS

ACKNOWLEDGMENTS

John of Salisbury, a twelfth-century theologian and author, wrote a treatise on logic in Latin, the language of scholars, in 1159. One of his statements has been translated as "We are dwarfs sitting on the shoulders of giants. We see more, and things that are more distant, than they did, not because our sight is superior or because we are taller than they, but because they raise us up, and by their great stature add to ours." That certainly applies in my case.

All investors and I owe large debts of gratitude to the investment giants I quote from in this book. The authors and publishers listed below have been generous in granting reprint permissions for the excerpts I have used from their works. I gratefully acknowledge their kindness and generosity in allowing me to share their insights with you. Without them this book would not exist.

Excerpts in this book used with permission from the authors and publishers are listed in the order in which they appear in this book as follows:

The Intelligent Investor—Revised Edition by Benjamin Graham, copyright 1973, published by HarperCollins Publishers, Inc.

I worked for months to track down the authors and publishers of all of the books cited, but in some instances I was unable to contact the proper parties. The insights of the authors quoted are so instructive that I felt they should be included in abbreviated form even if I could not secure outright permissions. I reduced my use of those excerpts to what

I understand the limits of fair use to be. I hope my use of the quotes is acceptable to all concerned.

I feel obliged to mention one other work that does not appear in this book but is a very worthwhile read for investors, both amateur and professional. The title is *Rediscovering the Wheel: Contrary Thinking & Investment Strategy* by Bradbury K. Thurlow, copyright 1981, published by Fraser Publishing Company. I recommend it to you for the author's wit as well as his insights on investing. If you have a specific question about an area of investing that I do not touch upon, you might look at www.investopedia.com, an encyclopedic website on the topic of investments.

I must acknowledge and publicly thank my sister, Alice Louise Goodwin; and my good friends, Sam Paque and Dennis Fitzpatrick, for their proofreading efforts. They saved me from myself many times. The wonderful folks at CreateSpace did a marvelous job of taking my manuscript and turning it into a book I can be proud of. Any mistakes you may find in the book are the result of my not taking their valuable advice.

A note of thanks is also due Susan Duval, who labored tirelessly to get this book typed and formatted in proper fashion in its early stages. Her expertise is exceeded only by her sense of humor and patience with me.

Finally, as all married writers should, I gratefully acknowledge the unfailing support of my wife, Mary Jo. I thank her for putting up with me and this book in its several iterations over the years it has taken to complete the work.

Miles Goodwin
Mill Creek, Washington
June, 2016

INTRODUCTION

In the 1995 movie *The Usual Suspects*, one of the main characters, Verbal Kint, quoted French writer Charles Baudelaire in describing the unknown archvillain in the movie. He said, "The greatest trick the devil ever pulled was convincing the world he did not exist." Similarly, the greatest trick Wall Street has ever pulled was convincing people they could not successfully invest their own money.

This book is a compilation and review of some of the best books on investing for individual investors, such as *The Art of Speculation* by Philip Carret, *Common Stocks and Uncommon Profits* by Philip Fisher, *The Intelligent Investor* by Benjamin Graham, *A Random Walk down Wall Street* by Burton Malkiel, *The Nature of Risk, Stock Market Survival and the Meaning of Life* by Justin Mamis, *The Money Game* by Adam Smith, and many others. With the help of these authors, you can learn how to invest your money successfully.

The folks offering investment services minimize their fees and charges by saying, "It's only one percent a year." That is true, but if you pay that seemingly small percentage every year over, say, a thirty-year investing career, it looks like you will have paid a cumulative 30 percent of your money to have someone do for you what you could have done for yourself. What you will learn from these books is that it is not that hard to match average market returns—something a significant percentage of investment professionals fail to do each year.

To become a confident and therefore successful investor, you should delve into the books I cite. If a particular excerpt in this book resonates with you, read the book that contains it. Each of them is much better written and certainly more enlightening than this one. However, this book is a start.

1

Language of Wall Street

A VOCABULARY LESSON

Almost every area of study has specialized terms. Medicine, law, engineering, and science all have their own vocabularies. Although unfamiliar to those outside the professions, they have meaning and significance to those within the fields. The same is true of investing. Those who want to invest must know the terms used on Wall Street. For readers familiar with investment/business terms, the following may be tedious and can be skipped, but I have to assume that some readers may not be familiar with Wall Street jargon. Vocabulary exercises tend to be boring, so we'll avoid the dictionary style of defining words. The business/investment terms you as an investor should understand will be highlighted in **bold** in the story below. The following is how a business comes into being.

Assume I have an idea for a new business. The only problem is that I don't have enough money to get it off the ground. I want to run a blog and charge people a subscription fee to read it. I will need an office; fast, powerful computers; servers to handle the traffic I expect to generate; professional help with the design and launch of the site; and employees to keep the site up and running. All of that takes money, or **capital**. No bank is going to lend me $5,000 to launch my dream. Therefore I have to find people who share my belief that the site can make a profit and want to own a piece of the business.

After badgering my friends and family, I get five people to commit to buying shares. They could be called **angel investors**, since their money seems almost heaven sent. However, not everyone is willing to invest an equal amount to raise the necessary $5,000. Some are willing to invest only $200 while others have more money to risk. I have $1,000 to put into the business. Having secured investment commitments, I file **Articles of Incorporation** for Best Blogs Ever, Inc. (BBE) with the state. The Articles authorize BBE to issue up to one thousand shares. Those shares are **authorized**. BBE will **issue** (sell to the investors) shares of its **common stock** for ten dollars per share. The initial price per share is called the stock's **par value**. The five hundred shares sold by the corporation at ten dollars each to the investors are now **outstanding**. Someone with $200 to invest will get twenty shares. I get one hundred shares for my $1,000 investment and so on with each of the other investors. Each investor owns a percentage of the corporation and its profits and losses equal to the percentage his or her cash investment represents of the total $5,000 of capital raised. This money is the **equity** in the company. Since the shareholders do not intend to participate in the operation of the business, they elect individuals who will control the business—the **board of directors**. The board oversees the business and elects **officers** for the corporation who will handle day-to-day details. Typically a corporation has a president, a vice president, a secretary, and a treasurer. There may be more officers, but these are the typical positions in a business.

My blogs are well received on the web. BBE earns $1,000 in its first year of business. **Gross revenue** is the term for all of the money paid by the subscribers to read the blogs. The obvious goal is for gross revenue to exceed all of the company's expenses consisting of rent, payroll, utilities, advertising, computer maintenance, taxes, and the like. Once those expenses are deducted from the revenue, the remaining funds are the company's **income** or **earnings**.

The shareholders want to know what the board of directors proposes to do with the earnings for the year. Since BBE might need some of the money in the future, the directors decide to keep half the earnings in the company and pay the shareholders a **dividend** of one dollar per share on the five hundred outstanding shares. Since each share was purchased for ten dollars and a one dollar dividend is paid per share, the **dividend rate** on the investment of the shareholders is 10 percent.

The $500 not paid out in dividends represents the company's **retained earnings**. Those retained earnings, which are one of the **assets** of BBE, have increased the value of BBE because the company has additional cash, the $500, in its bank account. If you add that money to the value of the $5,000 of initial capital, there is now $5,500 of equity shared by the five hundred shares. Technically, each share should now be worth eleven dollars. Another term for that worth is **book value**. A company's book value is the difference between the assets of the company and its **liabilities**, what the company owes to third parties. The first year of operations has been a success. BBE made money, increased its assets, and paid a dividend. From an accounting standpoint, the shareholders' investment has increased in book value.

I have now been blogging for several years, and every year BBE has generated earnings. However, this success has created problems. The increase in subscriber traffic has outstripped the capacity of the servers, resulting in slower downloads and complaints from subscribers about difficulties logging on to the site. As a result we are worried about losing subscribers. BBE needs more servers. The shareholders decide the company should issue more stock to raise the necessary capital to buy them. The existing shareholders might buy some of the stock, but to raise the entire amount needed, new investors must be found. Therefore BBE will approach a **venture capital firm**, which raises money from institutional investors such as pension funds, university endowment funds, and other sources with the capacity to invest millions of dollars. Once the funds are raised, the venture capitalists invest the capital in new, growing businesses.

The five original BBE shareholders want to retain control of the company. They do not want a venture capital investor to buy enough common stock to outvote them on business decisions. In this sort of situation, many corporations issue a different form of stock, one that does not have voting rights but does have some rights not enjoyed by the voting common stock. The nonvoting shares could have a preference over the voting shares in one way or another—in effect a trade-off of one right for another. This form of stock is called **preferred stock**.

We meet with representatives from a venture capital firm, Venture Funds, Inc. (VFI). Before the meeting VFI asked for copies of BBE's **financial statements** for each year of operation. Those financial statements consist of three different accounting reports: a balance sheet, a profit and loss or income statement, and a cash flow statement. A **balance sheet** shows the assets, liabilities, and equity of the company as of each year end. A **profit and loss or income statement** shows the gross revenue, expenses, and any profit or loss for each year. A **cash flow statement** shows the cash held by the company at the beginning of each year, the cash generated during the year from all sources (*e.g.*, operations, loans, stock sales and any other cash generators); the way cash was spent during the year (*e.g.*, the purchase of equipment or other assets, investments, loan payments and dividends); and the cash position of the company at year end. The financial statements provide the information needed to determine how a business is doing.

After several meetings VFI agrees to an investment in the form of a combination of preferred shares and common shares. VFI will own fewer common shares than the original shareholders. The preferred shares will have a fixed annual dividend that the company must pay before any dividends can be paid on common shares. This is a fairly common right granted to preferred stock holders. VFI's preferred shares will be **cumulative**, which means any unpaid dividends on the preferred shares must be repaid before the common shares receive any dividends. If BBE could not pay the preferred stock dividend for three consecutive years, then VFI would have the right to convert some or all of its preferred shares into common shares with voting rights. Their preferred shares, therefore, are also **convertible**. If VFI converts its preferred shares into common stock, it could elect its own board of directors, who would elect new officers and then control BBE and its operations.

With final agreement reached, the articles of incorporation are amended to authorize issuance of the needed additional shares, the legal papers are completed, and BBE receives VFI's money. BBE buys the servers and has them installed. However, this takes more time than expected. Because of the delays, the anticipated increase in revenues does not begin for many months after VFI's investment. Although BBE is able to maintain the same level of earnings during the expansion, the money is needed to support the increased operational costs. VFI's preferred share dividend is paid as required, but the board of directors decides they cannot prudently declare a cash dividend on the common shares. In other words, the directors would have to **pass the dividend** and keep the earnings in the company.

This is not the sort of news that shareholders want to receive. To provide some form of return to the shareholders, the board of directors declares a **stock dividend** on a three for two basis. Instead of a cash dividend, each shareholder receives one-half of a share of stock, *at no cost*, for each share he or she already owns. It may take some time for financial benefits to be realized from a stock dividend, but if BBE continues to prosper, extra cash dividends on the extra shares could be received in the future. For example, if prior to the stock dividend a BBE shareholder had one thousand shares and was entitled to a cash dividend of five cents a share, then he or she would receive fifty dollars. After the three for two stock dividend, that same shareholder would have 1,500 shares. That same five cents a share dividend, if reinstituted later on, would net the individual seventy-five dollars, a larger cash dividend. Typically, however, the dividend is proportionately reduced to accommodate the increased number of outstanding shares. A stock dividend, in most instances, is the same as a **stock split**. A stock dividend is an issuance of additional shares instead of cash. A stock split is simply an increase in the number of shares the company has issued, usually on a two for one basis. In either event, any later cash dividend is divided and spread over the original shares and the additional shares received by shareholders. A stock dividend has the same purpose as a cash dividend: to provide a return to shareholders. A stock split increases the number of shares, which lowers the price for a publicly traded stock. The company may want to lower its stock price to a desired trading range to encourage more people to buy the stock and increase its liquidity in the market.

Our staff now includes seven bloggers covering a total of twenty-eight different topics in as many blogs posted every week. There are many areas of interest we do not cover. We decided early on that if we could not provide a quality blog on a topic, we would not put out a second-rate post. We keep an eye on other sites posting on topics we do not address.

One such blog is operated by a company with offices in our city— Blogging Topics, Inc. (BTI). After some discussion with our board of directors about expanding our blog topics, I set up a meeting with the president of BTI to discuss combining our companies. BBE and BTI could enter into a **merger**. There are three ways for BBE to acquire BTI. BBE could pay BTI shareholders cash for their stock. The second way would involve a swap of BTI shares for BBE shares (common or preferred). The third option would be a combination of stock and cash for the BTI shares.

After negotiations we agree to a merger of BBE with BTI in the form of a stock swap of the common shares of BTI for **second series**

preferred shares to be issued by BBE. This series of preferred shares would be subordinate to the cumulative convertible preferred shares held by VFI. The second series would have slightly different rights. We agree that the BTI shareholders will exchange their common shares for a second series of cumulative preferred stock paying a fixed dividend plus an added feature. Although not convertible, the shares would be **participating**. A participating preferred share receives not only its declared dividend but also an additional dividend keyed off the dividend declared on the common shares of a company. Once the common share dividend reaches a certain level, the second series cumulative participating preferred shares will receive additional dividends, in effect participating in any additional dividend increases.

The second series of cumulative participating preferred shares represents a significant financial obligation for BBE. We want the option to reduce this liability in the future. We feel that if the preferred shares are participating, they should also be **callable**. This means that BBE can redeem these preferred shares at par value at some point in the future. This might happen if BBE could borrow money to buy back the shares at an interest rate lower than the dividend rate, resulting in a lower annual payment. This is acceptable to the BTI shareholders.

The merger is completed, and BBE is now a much larger company. As everyone hoped, things go well, and BBE continues to grow over the years. The added blogs result in more revenue and income. We increase our dividend each year, and we have every indication that our shareholders are very happy with their investment. Our success does not go unnoticed.

Our board of directors receives a letter from one of the large Internet companies, Gobble Corporation, asking if we have any interest in merging with them. Gobble is a publicly traded company with a history of acquiring small Internet companies. They have a blogging division and think BBE would be a nice fit. Gobble proposes to purchase

BBE at forty-five dollars per share of common stock, which we consider a lowball number.

When we tell Gobble we do not want to merge with them, they indicate they are not going to drop the matter and intend to mount a **hostile takeover**. A few weeks later, each of our shareholders receives a letter offering to buy their shares at a price slightly higher than the one Gobble had initially offered in their letter to our board. This type of direct offer to shareholders is called a **tender offer**. Gobble offers to pay fifty dollars per share to each shareholder if a majority of the shareholders accept the tender offer by a certain date. The offer is conditioned on Gobble acquiring enough shares in BBE to gain voting control of the company. As the date for acceptance of the tender offer nears, each side strongly lobbies the shareholders.

Ultimately Gobble does not gain control of our company through the tender offer, but it does manage to purchase VFI's common shares for fifty-five dollars per share plus all of its preferred shares in a private transaction. With Gobble's purchase of VFI's shares, the fox is now in the henhouse. Not unexpectedly, Gobble mounts a second effort to persuade the shareholders to throw in with it at the next annual shareholder meeting. They launch a **proxy fight** in the weeks before the meeting. Each shareholder has one vote for each share of stock he or she owns. If a shareholder cannot attend the shareholders' meeting but still wishes to vote, the votes could be cast by an individual authorized to vote them in the absent shareholder's name. Such a written authorization to vote shares is called a **proxy**. If Gobble is able to convince enough shareholders to give it their proxies and vote in a new slate of directors, Gobble could gain control of BBE without owning a majority of the voting shares.

As word of the fifty-five dollars paid by Gobble for each of VFI's common shares spreads among our shareholders, we have to face the fact that the idea of receiving such a profit on their stock would appeal to our longtime shareholders. We have only one alternative to offer our shareholders against Gobble's efforts: take BBE **public**. We argue that turning BBE into a **publicly traded company** would offer shareholders the opportunity to sell their long-held shares at a price that might be higher than the one Gobble offered them earlier. We warn them that if Gobble gains control of the board of directors and forces a merger, the price our shareholders might receive could be less than either the tender offer price or the price paid to VFI.

On the day of the shareholder meeting, we prevail. Gobble does not receive enough proxies to gain a majority of the votes. We now have to undertake the task of taking the company public in an **initial public offering** (IPO). We schedule a special shareholder meeting to discuss an IPO. The big question is the anticipated price of BBE stock. We explain that the price is set by the **investment bank** that helps BBE make a public offering of stock. An investment bank works with companies going public, unlike a **commercial bank**, that accepts deposits and makes loans. The investment bank we pick agrees to act as the **underwriter** for BBE's shares to be offered to the public. They review BBE's financial statements and determine what price BBE's stock might command in an IPO. They then offer to buy BBE's stock from the company at a price that is lower than the anticipated opening price to the public but acceptable to the shareholders. This difference in price is their compensation for handling the IPO. The underwriter will purchase all of the shares to be issued by BBE at the lower price and then resell those shares to the public at the higher IPO price on the day BBE goes public. BBE receives its money from the investment bank. The underwriter takes the risk that public investors will buy all of the offered shares at the IPO price. The price calculated by the investment bank is not the only factor that comes into play in an IPO.

The art of pricing the shares is also based on the investment company's years of experience and feel for the state of the market at the time of the IPO. A **bull market**, with steadily increasing stock prices, high daily trading volume, and strong investor interest in stocks, would bode well for a successful IPO. If the market at that time is a **bear market** with rapidly declining prices and overall market fear, the offering price would have to be set lower. Alternatively, the investment bankers may advise the company to postpone the IPO until a more favorable market returns.

As the date of the IPO approaches, everything seems to fall into place, with a great deal of market interest in BBE. The offering is a success. On the day of the IPO, investors in the market take all the shares, and BBE's stock begins trading on an exchange.

The purpose of this story has been to introduce you to various financial and investment terms you will meet in your investing career. Hopefully, learning these terms through the story of BBE has not been painfully boring. I patterned this vocabulary lesson on a similar story contained in an excellent investment book, *How to Buy Stocks,* written by Louis Engel in 1953. Since its initial publication, this book has gone through eight revised editions. In light of its continued publication over the last sixty-plus years, it is obvious that both beginning and veteran investors find this book a great resource.

2

Markets

B enjamin Graham gave the following description of stock markets in his investment classic *The Intelligent Investor*:

> Imagine that in some private business you own a small share that cost you $1,000. One of your partners, named Mr. Market, is very obliging indeed. Every day he tells you what he thinks your interest is worth and furthermore offers either to buy you out or to sell you an additional interest on that basis. Sometimes his idea of value appears plausible and justified by business developments and prospects as you know them. Often, on the other hand, Mr. Market lets his enthusiasm or his fears run away with him, and the value he proposes seems to you a little short of silly. If you are a prudent investor or a sensible businessman, will you let Mr. Market's daily communication determine your view of the value of a $1,000 interest in the enterprise? Only in case you agree with him or in case you want to trade with him. You may be happy to sell out to him when he quotes you a ridiculously high price, and equally happy to buy from him when his price is low. But the rest of the time you will be wiser to form your own ideas of the value of your holdings, based on

full reports from the company about its operations and financial position.[1]

And, as they say, no one has ever said it any better.

There are two things to take away from Mr. Graham's analysis of Mr. Market. First, the price quotes in the stock market are transitory, changing by the minute. Second, an individual investor should never confuse price with value.

HANGING WITH THE WRONG CROWD

Adam Smith is a pseudonym for George J. W. Goodman, an award-winning financial author. *The Money Game*, one of several books he has written on investing and the stock market, provides an entertaining, insider look at Wall Street and the antics of the people who populate it. He likens the millions of investors in the stock market to a crowd. To support his proposition, he calls upon Charles Mackay, who wrote about crowd madness in 1841, and Gustave Le Bon, a French physician who studied the phenomenon of crowds in 1895. This is what Adam Smith had to say about Mr. Mackay and Dr. Le Bon:

> In 1841 David (Charles) Mackay published what is supposed to be the first good book on crowds, Extraordinary Popular Delusions and the Madness of Crowds. Mr. Mackay's book, said Mr. Bernard M. Baruch, helped him make his fortune and one Wall Street investment house sends the book out as a Christmas present. If any of its clients read the book, they probably felt superior, because those Dutchmen who kept bidding the prices of tulips higher and higher a couple of centuries ago now seem sort of silly. Unfortunately, it is quite possible to read about Dutchmen thinking that the world has an infinite hunger for

tulips, and then to go right out and buy some snazzy computer stock because the world has an infinite hunger for computers. There must always be a rationale, and if the computer rationale is easier than the tulip rationale, it may just be that we do not know the whole story on tulips.

At the end of the nineteenth century, a French physician called Gustave Le Bon published his Psychologie des Foules, translated as The Crowd. To Le Bon, a crowd was not merely a number of people assembled in one place; it could be thousands of isolated individuals. These he called a psychological crowd, subject to "the disappearance of conscious personality and the turning of feelings and thoughts in a different direction." According to Le Bon, the sentiments and ideas of all persons in a gathering take one and the same direction, and their conscious personality vanishes. A collective mind is formed, doubtless transitory, but presenting very clearly defined characteristics. The gathering has then become a psychological crowd. In such situations, the actions of the individuals may be quite different from those the same individuals would consider when alone. One of the most striking features of the crowd to Le Bon was its great difficulty in separating the imagined from the real. "A crowd thinks in images, and the image itself calls up a series of other images, having no logical connection with the first...a crowd scarcely distinguishes between the subjective and the objective."

Le Bon was an astute, if not particularly sympathetic, observer of crowds, and his description of crowd behavior is strikingly applicable to what we can readily discover taking place in financial markets.[2]

We will study these two authors next.

FLOWERS THROUGH THE CENTURIES

In 1841 Charles Mackay wrote his classic *Memoirs of Extraordinary Popular Delusions and the Madness of Crowds*. In addition to other forms of crowd madness, he described the Holland tulip market in 1636. The tulip bubble is most often cited in popular literature as the poster child for a market gone mad. As you chuckle over the antics of the normally sober Dutch back then, substitute the words *Internet companies* for *tulips*. If you tracked the wild stock market at the close of the twentieth century, you will see that the only difference in the two markets is 360-plus years. The behavior of the people is remarkably similar, as were the ultimate results. Here are excerpts from Mr. Mackay's work:

THE TULIPOMANIA

Quis furor, o cives!—Lucan.

The tulip—so named, it is said, from a Turkish word, signifying a turban—was introduced into western Europe about the middle of the sixteenth century. Conrad Gesner, who claims the merit of having brought it into repute,-little dreaming of the commotion it was shortly afterwards to make in the world,-says that he first saw it in the year 1559, in a garden at Augsburg, belonging to the learned Counsellor Herwart, a man very famous in his day for his collection of rare exotics.

The demand for tulips of a rare species increased so much in the year 1636, that regular marts for their sale were established on the Stock exchange of Amsterdam, in Rotterdam, Harlaem, Leyden, Alkmar, Hoorn, and other towns. Symptoms of gambling now became, for the first time, apparent. The stock-jobbers, ever on the alert for a new speculation, dealt largely in tulips, making use of all the means they so well knew how to employ to cause fluctuations in prices. At first, as in all these gambling mania, confidence was at its height, and every body gained. Many individuals grew suddenly rich. A golden bait hung temptingly out before the people, and one after the other, they rushed to the tulip-marts, like flies around a honey-pot. Every one imagined that the passion for tulips would last for ever, and that the wealthy from every part of the world would send to Holland, and pay whatever prices were asked for them. People of all grades converted their property into cash, and invested it in flowers. Foreigners became smitten with the same frenzy, and money poured into Holland from all directions.

At last, however, the more prudent began to see that this folly could not last for ever. Rich people no longer bought the flowers to keep them in their gardens, but to sell them again at cent per cent profit. It was seen that somebody must lose fearfully in the end. As this conviction spread, prices fell, and never rose again. Confidence was destroyed, and a universal panic seized upon the dealers. Many who, for a brief season, had emerged from the humbler walks of life, were cast back into their original obscurity. Substantial merchants were reduced almost to beggary, and many a representative of a noble line saw the fortunes of his house ruined beyond redemption.[3]

Professor Robert J. Shiller, a Yale economics professor, author, and Nobel Laureate, discussed the tulip bubble in his 2000 book *Irrational Exuberance*. He argued that it was not necessarily an example of irrational behavior. Shiller examined the records of price action of tulip bulbs then and compared it to the price action of stocks in today's markets. He found marked similarities between the bidding for bulbs by the Dutch back then and the bidding for stocks by investors today; the only apparent difference being the asset traded.

LE BON'S BONBONS

Dr. Gustave Le Bon's analysis of crowds in his 1895 book *The Crowd, A Study of the Popular Mind* is as pertinent today as it was at the end of the nineteenth century. He described a crowd as follows:

In its ordinary sense the word "crowd" means a gathering of individuals of whatever nationality, profession, or sex, and whatever be the chances that have brought them together. From the psychological point of view, the expression "crowd" assumes quite a different signification. The gathering has thus become what, in the absence of a better expression, I will call an organized crowd, or, if the term is considered preferable, a psychological crowd. It forms a single being, and is subjected to the law of the mental unity of crowds.

The disappearance of conscious personality and the turning of feelings and thoughts in a definite direction, which are the primary characteristics of a crowd about to become organized, do not always involve the simultaneous presence of a number of individuals on one spot. Thousands of isolated individuals may acquire at certain moments, and under the influence of certain violent emotions—such, for example, as a great national event—the characteristics of a psychological crowd. The psychological crowd is a provisional being formed of heterogeneous elements, which for a moment are combined, exactly as the cells which constitute a living body form by their reunion a new being which displays characteristics very different from those possessed by each of the cells singly. What really takes place is a combination followed by the creation of new characteristics, just as in chemistry certain elements, when brought into contact—bases and acids for example—combine to form a new body possessing properties quite different from those of the bodies that served to form it.[4]

He went on to describe the characteristics of people caught up in a psychological crowd:

If the individuals of a crowd confined themselves to putting in common the ordinary qualities of which each of them has his share, there would merely result the striking of an average, and not, as we have said is actually the case, the creation of new characteristics. How is it that these new characteristics are created? This is what we are now to investigate.

The first is that the individual forming part of a crowd acquires, solely from numerical considerations, a sentiment of invincible power which allows him to yield to instincts which, had he been alone, he would perforce have kept under restraint. He will be the less disposed to check himself from the consideration that, a crowd being anonymous, and in consequence irresponsible, the sentiment of responsibility which always controls individuals disappears entirely.

The second cause, which is contagion, also intervenes to determine the manifestation in crowds of their special characteristics, and at the same time the trend they are to take. In a crowd every sentiment and act is contagious, and contagious to such a degree that an individual readily sacrifices his personal interest to the collective interest.

A third cause, and by far the most important, determines in the individuals of a crowd special characteristics which are quite contrary at times to those presented by the isolated individual. I allude to that suggestibility of which, moreover, the contagion mentioned above is neither more nor less than an effect.

An individual in a crowd is a grain of sand amid other grains of sand, which the wind stirs up at will.[5]

Justin Mamis described the market in terms of sand and waves instead of wind in his book *The Nature of Risk, Stock Market Survival and the Meaning of Life*:

A useful simile for the stock market might be that of the tide, waves and a beach. The tide comes in and goes out in cyclical fashion; the waves come in and go out like market fluctuations, but in differing fashions—crashing, gentle, white-capped, mild. Each wave, each tide, affects the grains of sand on the beach, shifting them here and there; there may be a period of erosion, a period of rebuilding, but in a different place. Those shifting grains of sand make up the (long term) beach, just as constantly shifting but minute changes in price, tick by tick, make up the stock market.[6]

THANK YOU, MR. DOW

What exactly is a stock market? What exactly is a stock market index? The short answer would be that a stock market and its index can be whatever you want them to be. You could say a stock market is composed of thousands of publicly traded companies traded on many stock exchanges. You then pick a group of those stocks to form an index that will give you a representation of that stock market's general movement. The goal of a stock market index is to contain a group of stocks that accurately correlates with and reflects the general movement of all of the stocks traded in a particular market. Today, the three most recognizable stock market indices are the Standard & Poor's 500 (S&P 500), the National Association of Securities Dealers Automated Quotations (NASDAQ), and the grandfather of them all, the Dow Jones Industrial Average (DJIA). When people ask, "What did the market do today?" they generally expect to hear what happened to the DJIA.

Charles Dow published his first stock average in 1884. It highlighted growth stocks of the time. His first benchmark average included nine railroads, a steamship company, and Western Union (all considered "high tech" at the time). In May 1896 Dow converted these original stocks into his Transportation Average and created his first Industrial Average, based on twelve companies. General Electric, one of the original industrial companies, was organized by Thomas Edison in 1890 and remains part of the average to this day. Although the companies changed over the years, the DJIA included only twelve stocks until 1916, when it was increased to twenty companies. The number increased to thirty in January 1929, where it has remained ever since. The 1929 average included some companies still recognized today, such as General Motors, B. F. Goodrich, Sears Roebuck (now Sears Holdings Corp.), Westinghouse, and U.S. Steel, all of which are no longer in the average.

In January 1900 the smaller average (twelve stocks) was 68.13. It took until 1920 for the DJIA to first break one hundred. It peaked at 307.01 in January 1929 (then thirty stocks) before plunging after the stock market crash and subsequent depression to a low of 41.22 in 1932. The average remained in the one hundreds from 1934 until December 1949, when it closed over two hundred. It did not break one thousand until 1972 but seesawed thereafter until the beginning of the roughly eighteen-year bull market in 1982. The Dow went on to surpass two thousand in 1987 and three thousand in 1991. The bull market continued with the DJIA breaking four thousand in February 1995 and five thousand nine months later. It went above six thousand in 1996 and crossed the eleven thousand mark in 1999. The subsequent market drop, starting in 2000, lowered the average, and it did not recover to its previous high until 2006. Subsequent market increases and falls continued until November 2013, when the DJIA first crossed sixteen thousand. The index closed, for the first time, above seventeen thousand in July 2014 and above eighteen thousand in February 2015.

The Dow's reaching each benchmark of one thousand points piques the interest of the public and garners media attention. However, most experienced investors recognize that it is just that—interesting but not really significant from a financial standpoint.

MARKET CYCLES—MICROSCOPES, TELESCOPES, AND SATELLITES

These three tools are used to look at things but each for a different purpose. Microscopes let us focus on objects invisible to the naked eye. Telescopes enable us to view faraway things in sharp detail. Satellites provide clear pictures of our Earth. Each instrument is used to view objects at a different distance for a different purpose. Like most tools, if not used correctly, they are of little help. I would like to analogize them to tools used in making investments. In my analogy, we are concerned with time and market cycles, not distance.

A trader looking for a quick profit will study the detailed movement of a stock, much like a scientist might look through a microscope at a specimen slide. Based on hourly, daily, or weekly price movement, the short-term speculator, or day trader, plots a stock's future direction and invests based on that forecasted movement. Al Frank pointed out in his book, *Al Frank's New Prudent Speculator*, that the shorter the time period being examined, the more likely the movement will be random. Justin Mamis wrote the following about short-term trading in his 1994 book *When to Sell—Inside Strategies for Stock-Market Profits*:

Just as long-term investors pooh-pooh market swings as not affecting **them**, short term traders exaggerate the significance of every little twitch, convinced that looking at the market through a microscope will disclose its secrets. **This need has been intensified by what seems, to such traders, to be the almost magical solution— that is, computers**.

These tick by tick, or moment-to-moment charts have all the appearance of reality, and can, indeed, be "read" the same way as a daily or weekly chart...so the trader believes in them far beyond their usefulness. They cause over-trading, and all losses lead from **that**. They create a belief that one knows what one is doing, when it is really the **noise** of the trading floor and trading rooms around the country that one is staring at.[7] [Author's emphasis in **bold**.]

An individual with a longer time line may be able to avoid some of the randomness of daily price movements. The long-term investor could be thought of as looking through a telescope at a more distant time horizon. However, a longer-term investor/speculator investing not on financial statistics but on a Wall Street story about a company and the expected success of its product or service may not be much safer than one who is trading on random action.

Adam Smith, in *The Money Game*, recounted a couple of sad but true stock stories:

In 1961 the whole world was going to go bowling, but in 1962 Brunswick managed to make it from 74 to 8 with scarcely a skid mark. In 1965 the whole world was going to sit and watch color television, but shortly thereafter Admiral, Motorola, Zenith and Magnavox collapsed like a soufflé on which the oven door has been untimely slammed. It will happen again.[8]

One of the more famous eras of story investing occurred in the 1970s and was based on the idea of never-ending growth. Wall Street professionals and individual investors became mesmerized by a group of large capitalization stocks on the New York Stock Exchange known as the "nifty fifty," whose earnings and, therefore, stock prices were expected to rise for the foreseeable future.

The last instrument is the satellite, which gives a global perspective in distances. In our time-horizon analogy, the satellite might cover many years, if not decades, of market action. A well-known long-term cycle was developed by a Russian economist, Nikolai Dmitriyevich Kondratieff. It bears his name—the Kondratieff wave. This cycle, or wave, covers a period of up to fifty years from beginning to end and is meant to expose major moves in commodity prices. It is also supposed to explain boom and bust cycles in capitalistic countries. I would point out that the investing careers of most individuals will probably not last for a complete fifty-year Kondratieff wave.

Ralph Nelson Elliott, an accountant, believed market prices moved in specific patterns based on prevailing crowd psychology, alternating between optimism and pessimism. Mr. Elliott explained his theory, popularly referred to as the Elliott wave, in his book *The Wave Principle* in 1938. He identified a five-wave pattern and a three-wave pattern, each of which reveals market patterns based on sequences of Fibonacci numbers. Interestingly, sequences of these Fibonacci numbers can also be seen in growth patterns found throughout nature.

Norman G. Fosback reviewed several cyclical theories in his book *Stock Market Logic, A Sophisticated Approach to Profits on Wall Street*. He concluded his study with this observation:

Most cycles are without doubt figments of the imagination. Nevertheless, strange things exist in the universe, and the ultimate resolution of the truth of cyclic phenomena must await future study. In the meantime, if cycles have a utility, it is in reminding us that "This, too, shall pass;" that no bull market or bear market lasts forever.[9]

RANDOM MARKETS

We turn our attention to the random walk market theory. I want to start with a passage from a book by Professor Stephen Jay Gould, a paleontologist and essayist who wrote extensively about paleontology, evolution, and the history of science. In *Full House, The Spread of Excellence from Plato to Darwin*, he discussed how humans cope with trends and randomness in life, which he then extended to the stock market:

> The more important the subject and the closer it cuts to the bone of our hopes and needs, the more we are likely to err in establishing a framework for analysis. We are story-telling creatures, products of history ourselves. We are fascinated by trends, in part because they tell stories by the basic device of imparting directionality to time, in part because they so often support a moral dimension to a sequence of events; a cause to bewail as something goes to pot, or to highlight as a rare beacon of hope.
>
> As one final example, probably more intellectual energy has been invested in discovering (and exploiting) trends in the stock market than in any other subject—for the obvious reason that the stakes are so high, as measured in the currency of our culture. The fact that no one has ever come close to finding a consistent way to beat the system—despite intense efforts by some of the smartest people in the world—probably indicates that such causal trends do not exist, and that the sequences are effectively random.[10]

The efficient market hypothesis (EMH), also known as the random walk theory, is based on a doctoral thesis written by a French mathematician, Louis Bachelier, in 1900, entitled *The Theory of Speculation*. Bachelier studied the degree of fluctuation in stock prices and constructed a set of mathematical equations that demonstrated that the variations in price are proportional to the length of time in which those variations occur. His equations resulted in the finding that the range of fluctuations (up or down) was linked to the square root of the time interval of the fluctuations.

Bachelier wrote the following about market movements:

> Past, present, and even discounted future events are reflected in market price, but often show no apparent relation to price changes...[A]rtificial causes also intervene: the Exchange reacts on itself, and the current fluctuation is a function, not only of the previous fluctuations, but also of the current state. The determination of these fluctuations depends on an infinite number of factors; it is, therefore, impossible to aspire to mathematical predictions of it...[T]he dynamics of the Exchange will never be an exact science.[11]

Bachelier followed his thesis to its logical conclusion: the probability of a price rise is the same as the probability of a price decline at any given moment in time. He stated, "Clearly the price considered most likely by the market is the true current price: if the market judged otherwise, it would quote not this price, but another price higher or lower."[12]

Peter L. Berstein was an economist, university educator, investment manager, and famous author of several books on finance. In his 1992 book *Capital Ideas/The Improbable Origins of Modern Wall Street*, Berstein wrote the following about Bachelier:

The key to Bachelier's insight is his observation, expressed in a notably modern manner, that "contradictory opinions concerning [market] changes diverge so much that at the same instant buyers believe in a price increase and sellers believe in a price decrease." Convinced that there is no basis for believing that— on the average—either sellers or buyers consistently know any more about the future than the other, he arrived at an astonishing conjecture: "It seems that the market, the aggregate of speculators, **at a given instant**, can believe in neither a market rise nor a market fall, since, for each quoted price, there are as many buyers as sellers."[13] [Author's emphasis in **bold**.]

Bachelier's dissertation was "discovered" by Professor Paul Samuelson, an MIT economist and Nobel Laureate. Although it is reported that Professor Eugene F. Fama, a University of Chicago economist, first coined the term *random walk*, Professor Burton G. Malkiel brought it into the popular consciousness with his first edition of *A Random Walk Down Wall Street*. Professor Malkiel described the EMH in these terms:

A random walk is one in which future steps or directions cannot be predicted on the basis of past actions. When the term is applied to the stock market, it means that short-run changes in stock prices cannot be predicted. Investment advisory services, earnings predictions, and complicated chart patterns are useless. On Wall Street, the term "random walk" is an obscenity. It is an epithet coined by the academic world and hurled insultingly at the professional soothsayers. Taken to its logical extreme, it means that a blindfolded monkey throwing darts at a newspaper's financial pages could select a portfolio that would do just as well as one carefully selected by the experts.

The "narrow" (weak) form of the theory says that technical analysis—looking at past stock prices—could not help investors. The "broad" (semi-strong and strong) forms state that fundamental analysis is not helpful either: All that is known concerning the expected growth of the company's earnings and dividends, all of the possible favorable and unfavorable developments affecting the company that might be studied by the fundamental analyst, is already reflected in the price of the company's stock.[14]

In his book Bernstein points out that the stock price variations over time shown by Bachelier's equations are eerily similar to the action of molecules crashing into each other, which is known in physics as Brownian motion. It is indeed humbling to think that the prices generated by human beings in the market resemble the movement of molecules in nature.

The following is an argument for market randomness. Assume you have assembled five thousand people for a reality TV show, which you will call *The Flip*. With Hollywood hype and buildup, when you flip a coin, each contestant presses a button for either heads or tails. Like the NCAA year-end basketball tournament (March Madness), this is a "win or go home" competition. Each week, after the obviously random flip, the people who hit the wrong buttons leave the program. The process continues, and sooner or later a handful of survivors will have made a surprising, seemingly skillful string of correct calls. They may gain some degree of notoriety and celebrity status in the popular media, which you would hope for as the producer of the program. As these things go, finally there is only one person left—the winner. Does that individual indeed possess some innate talent for calling coin flips? Conversely, is it all just luck and the fact that someone will win, given the rules? Much is made of winning streaks of every sort in popular culture. What if it is all the result of chance and luck?

IS THAT A BOOM I HEAR?

In 1940 author Fred Schwed, Jr. wrote a hilarious account of Wall Street titled *Where Are the Customers'Yachts? or A Good Hard Look at Wall Street*. He worked on Wall Street for only a couple of years in the 1920s, but he apparently figured out its foibles and eccentricities in that short time. As Schwed saw it, there were not that many *utility maximizing agents* (an economist's term for investors) on the Street when he was there. He summarized Wall Street's appetite for market booms:

> In attempting to find out just what, if anything, was good in the good old days it is necessary to determine when the good old days were. In some simple, but not straightforward, Wall Street minds, they were any days that preceded the Securities and Exchange Commission, when there weren't no ten commandments and a man could raise a thirst. Oh for the days when the most important rules were "Don't rebate on commissions," "Don't shoot the specialists," and "Don't smoke opium on the floor during trading hours."
>
> It would be more correct and more honest to recognize that the good old days were simply boom days, like the booms of the late twenties, the late teens and the late nineteenth century.
>
> In our moments of sober thought we all realize that booms are bad things, not good. But nearly all of us have a secret hankering for another one. "Another little orgy wouldn't do us any harm," is the feeling that persists both downtown and up. This is quite human, because in the last boom we acted so silly. If we are old enough we probably acted silly in the last three. We either got in too late, or out too late, or both. But now that we are experienced, just give us one more shot at a good reliable runaway boom![15]

Yale professor and Nobel Laureate Robert J. Shiller described the three bull markets of the twentieth century in America in his best seller *Irrational Exuberance*. The bull market of the 1920s ended with the crash of 1929. The second bull market, spanning the 1950s and 1960s, ended with the market meltdown in 1973 and 1974. The third started in the early 1980s and was still going strong at the time his book was published.

Shiller's work hit bookstores in March 2000, the month during which the last-mentioned bull market hit its peak. In a 2001 afterword to the paperback edition of *Irrational Exuberance*, Professor Shiller described how, despite the severe drop in stock prices in the months following publication of his book, people still believed the market would ultimately resume its eighteen-year rise. As we know, market results over the next few years proved them wrong—very wrong.

A MARKET REPRISE—LE BON AND MAMIS

Both Dr. Le Bon and Justin Mamis used the analogy of grains of sand when writing about markets. Wind blows the sand around on a beach, much like individuals in Le Bon's market crowd. Waves move the sand to remake the beach, like the market for Mr. Mamis. It behooves the individual investor to keep these analogies in mind as he or she approaches investment choices.

Dr. Le Bon believed that a person in a crowd (either real or psychological) loses his or her sense of individual responsibility and becomes susceptible to the contagion of the idea or image embraced by the crowd. In effect the person becomes subject to a level of suggestibility that draws him or her ever deeper into the crowd. Once subject to the force of the crowd, the person loses control and adopts the crowd's vision with abandon.

Mr. Mamis said that each person has inner voices warning him or her of the risks in life and suggesting they be avoided. Careful thought and preparation for every risk in life is the inner parental caution.

Unfortunately neither life nor the market will always give a person sufficient time to fully ponder the choices or all of the information needed to make the best choice. As Mr. Mamis explained about the market, "Because it is a process, there is no one moment or single point, at which one can make an obvious 'sure' decision."[16]

So, what is the lesson? Remember the images of sand being moved about on a beach by either wind or waves, as depicted by Dr. Le Bon and Mr. Mamis. If you can do that, you may be able to reduce the pressures you will likely experience in the hurly-burly of the market and invest on your own terms.

Investors

FINDING YOUR INNER INVESTOR

To be an investor, you must recognize how you approach risk (your risk tolerance). Although you probably do not remember your first encounter with risk, rest assured that your parents' warnings are still buried in your memory. And like your parents back then, those cautions are guiding your actions today. Justin Mamis, an executive at the New York Stock Exchange and a specialist in technical analysis for many years, wrote *The Nature of Risk, Stock Market Survival and the Meaning of Life* in 1991. Mr. Mamis goes back to the beginning to explain risk and markets and how we approach them, each in our own way. Here are excerpts:

> The first word parents want a baby to understand and respond to is not Mama or Daddy—it's No. How is anyone going to learn to venture, to take a risk, when "No" resounds? Parents and baby may exchange smiles, but as soon as the baby wants to take a risk—that is, do something venturesome—the infant hears: "Don't touch that," "Watch out," "Be careful." From infancy's earliest days, taking a risk becomes a negative concept. "Don't" becomes a family motto. An infant knows no risk; all is ahead. Parents know all is risk, and try to protect. The child

learns what the parents teach, and a world that starts out full of possibilities becomes full of limits and danger.

We grow up in such a pervasive atmosphere of caution that it becomes astounding when we read about, or see, someone who actually does take risks willingly, skillfully, successfully. And even more astonishing: there actually are a few people who never consider risk at all; they just do. How does one become able to venture forward without anxiety? How does one use risk positively? When all is risk, as war is, or the street, or cancer, there is no future. "What the hell" derives from that sense, in contrast to a more standard "The future is at risk" so "Be careful." Thus it is the fear of the future that risk magnifies.[1]

What is it about risk that can be used to help the individual investor improve his or her return in the stock market? Here is Mr. Mamis's answer:

Let's examine one daily life situation—crossing the street—to see what the risks are. When risk is examined in terms of the moment-to-moment decisions—stepping off the curb being an assumption of risk with all the dictionary negatives of hazard, peril, exposure to danger, but also with a positive: to get successfully to the other side—risk is at its core making a decision.

Although infinitely more complex, the stock market is more like crossing the street. The stock market is as moment-to-moment within a long-term trend as life is. People think: I'm buying this house to live in while the babies grow up and go off to college; I'm marrying this person "till death do us part"—long term investments but moment-to-moment decisions. We get caught up in emotions, and believe our feelings represent our judgment about the long-term values. Thus there is a distinction between the religion of long-term beliefs, hopes and expectations, and the secular short-term practice of our moment-to-moment behavior. Although we might be convinced that the decisions we make have that long-term basis, they stem from the moment.

When a decision is required, the way we take information in, and how we use it, affects that decision. Our self's style goes back deep into childhood. The manner in which we let information in, our ability to understand it, to deal with it, and perhaps even distort it, all start with who we are, as developed from the moment of beginning, on our hands and knees, to explore the world. Thus the risk we are about to take via our next decision is not a simple choice of "do it or not" or "yes or no." Before deciding, we need to know why what we know is never enough, a question that, in turn, leads to what kind of information do we believe or trust?

But when information is insufficient we need the trust and belief in ourselves, and the inner acceptance that we'll be okay anyhow. We need the discipline to accept whatever is available. We need the experience to understand all the ifs, ands, and buts, and yet still confront the risk and make the decision. Setting ourselves free from the quest for information, oddly enough, is what reduces risk even as it appears from the freedom itself that risk is being scarily increased. Oh my, freedom; that's dangerous.[2]

To learn more about your own risk tolerance, you can take the online risk tolerance quiz created by Professor John E. Grable of University of Georgia, Athens and Professor Ruth H. Lytton of Virginia Tech University at http:// njaes.rutgers.edu:8080//money/riskquiz/. They have graciously allowed me to reprint the quiz with the scoring grid in the Appendix, but I would ask you to take the online quiz as well to assist them in their ongoing research into personal finance.

THE LONE WOLF

In some instances, when a wolf pup reaches maturity (around two years old), the leader of the pack, the alpha wolf, may see it as a threat to its leadership and drive it away. After that the lone wolf must look out for itself, without the support and companionship of the pack. Similarly a child eventually grows up and moves out to make his or her way in life. An investor should pattern his or her investing methods along the lines of the lone wolf. You must get comfortable making your own decisions and investment choices. You must learn not only to ignore the clamoring of the crowd but also to lower the volume on your subconscious whispers from childhood.

There are many investment strategies: fundamental analysis, including value, growth, and contrarian styles of investing; and technical analysis, including charts, market cycles and momentum trading, to name but a few. You can confidently invest once you find an investment strategy that makes sense to you and works best for you over time.

Aswath Damodaran, a professor of finance in the Stern School of Business at New York University, summed this up in his book *Investment Philosophies* with the following:

An investment philosophy represents a set of core beliefs about how investors behave and how markets work. To be a successful investor, you not only have to consider the evidence from the markets, but you also have to examine your own strengths and weaknesses to come up with an investment philosophy that best suits you. Investors without core beliefs tend to wander from strategy to strategy, drawn by anecdotal evidence or recent success, creating transaction costs and incurring losses as a consequence. Investors with clearly defined investment philosophies tend to be more consistent and disciplined in their investment choices.[3]

Wolves instinctively hunt in a pack. The lone wolf learns to hunt alone. Once the individual investor develops a personal investment strategy, he or she will find the self-confidence to also hunt alone.

WHO THE HELL ARE YOU?

Although I would probably be laughed out of the room by most movie critics, I like Arnold Schwarzenegger movies. Arnold is best known for the Terminator trilogy, in which he plays a relentless robot from the future. In one of his other roles, he played a special ops commando battling an alien in the 1987 sci-fi movie *Predator*. At the end of the movie, he, of course, has defeated the grotesque alien. Standing over the dying creature, he asks, "Who the hell are you?" The extraterrestrial, with its last dying breath, throws the question back at him.

You should ask yourself that question with respect to your investment strategy. In your forays into the stock market, are you an investor, a speculator, or a gambler? Philip Carret, Benjamin Graham, and Al Frank all discuss these distinctions in their books.

Philip Carret viewed investors, speculators, and gamblers on a continuum. In his book, *The Art of Speculation*, he distinguished between them as follows:

> "Your articles deal with speculative investment rather than with speculation," said an astute observer of both fields of activity when he had read the greater part of this book in serial form. To this charge the writer was forced to plead guilty. After all, it is by no means easy to draw the line between investment and

speculation, between speculation and gambling. If one is to discuss the topic of speculation and perhaps thereby induce some readers to attempt it who might otherwise have left speculation alone, it is much more helpful to the average reader, much less dangerous to the reader who might misinterpret what he reads, to discuss the sort of speculation which is on the borderland of investment than the more dangerous and less useful type of speculation which borders on gambling.[4]

Mr. Carret believed the difference between investment and speculation was the investor's motive. Was the individual looking for quick profit (speculation) or long-term appreciation (investment)?

Benjamin Graham was strict in his distinction between investment and speculation. In the opening paragraphs of *The Intelligent Investor*, he wrote, "An investment operation is one which, upon thorough analysis, promises safety of principal and an adequate return. Operations not meeting these requirements are speculative."[5]

He did concede that there could be intelligent speculation as well as intelligent investment; however, he did not waiver from the differences he saw between the two forms of market operation.

Al Frank, author of *Al Frank's New Prudent Speculator*, believed the difference between investment and speculation was more semantics than investment strategy. He cited a dictionary definition of speculation: "Engagement in any business transaction involving considerable risk for the chance of large gains."[6]

In contrast he pointed out that the same dictionary defined investment as follows: "The investing of money or capital for profitable returns."[7]

Frank noted the absence of the words *risk*, *chance*, and *large gains* in the definition of *investment*, which reflects an obvious bias: speculation equals risk, and investment equals safety. He totally disagreed with this distinction and maintained that all investing is essentially speculation.

The point of this discussion is to suggest that you, as an individual investor, must ask yourself this question. Regardless of how you may define the words, are you thinking like an investor, a speculator, or a gambler? No matter if you are looking for long-term appreciation or a quick, speculative profit, you should always leave the gambling for Las Vegas, not Wall Street.

WANNA BET?

As discussed above, one of the first steps in formulating an investment strategy is deciding what making an investment means to you. Is it all about investing your money in a well-run, publicly traded corporation? Or is it more like placing a bet at a blackjack table in Vegas? You need to know which type of investor you are. In *The Money Game*, Adam Smith wrote about the legendary English economist and investor John Maynard Keynes:

> We are taught—at least those of us who grew up without a great deal of it—that money is A Very Serious Business, that the stewardship of capital is holy, and that the handler of money must conduct himself as a Prudent Man. It is all part of the Protestant ethic and the spirit of Capitalism and I suppose it all helped to make this country what it is. Penny saved, penny earned, waste not, want not, Summer Sale, Save 10 Percent, and so on. Then I came across this sentence in "Long-Term Expectation" of Keynes' General Theory:
>
> "The game of professional investment is intolerably boring and overexacting to anyone who is entirely exempt from the gambling instinct; whilst he who has it must pay to this propensity the appropriate toll."

Game? Game? Why did the Master say Game? He could have said business or profession or occupation or what have you. What is a Game? It is "sport, play, frolic, or fun"; "a scheme or art employed in the pursuit of an object of purpose"; "a contest, conducted according to set rules, for amusement or recreation or winning a stake." Does that sound like Owning a Share of American Industry? Participating in the Long-Term Growth of the American Economy? No, but it sounds like the stock market.[8]

Justin Mamis also discussed the gambling aspects of stock investing in his book *The Nature of Risk, Stock Market Survival and the Meaning of Life*. He compared an investor to a sports fan in search of excitement:

The cliches of daily life are those of routine, discouragement, tiredness; of the rat race; of a cold, the IRS. Guys root for dreadful teams for years—keep buying season tickets in the hope that eventually they'll own seats for the Super Bowl or World Series. And better than being a sports fan—because you can actually participate—and even better than gambling—because it is socially acceptable—playing the stock market becomes a way out of an otherwise mundane and stressful environment. It has glamour, plus the chance of improving one's lot without being an overt bet. There's an excitement to it, along with the illusion that a successful investment is almost within reach, if one only knew how to use it. The market seems to represent hope itself.[9]

Buying stock in a company, regardless of the amount of study and careful investigation, remains, at its essence, a wager on the future performance of the company and its stock. A purchase of stock is basically a bet no matter how you dress it up.

GOT GAME?

What are the traits of an investor and a trader of securities? What type of person devotes his or her time to this activity? What is the attraction?

In *The Money Game*, Adam Smith described game theory, the mathematical study of actions in a multiple option conflict system (what Smith called the Game), which was developed by John von Neumann and Oskar Morgenstern in their 1944 seminal work, *A Theory of Games and Economic Behavior*. Smith then returned to his characterization of market denizens:

> I bring this up only because I think the market is both a game and a Game, i.e., both sport, frolic, fun, and play, and a subject for continuously measurable options. If it is a game, then we can relieve ourselves of some of the heavy and possibly crippling emotions that individuals carry into investing, because in a game the winning of the stake is clearly defined.
>
> If you are a player in the Game, or are thinking of becoming one, there is one irony of which you should be aware. The object of the game is to make money, hopefully a lot of it. All the players in the Game are getting rapidly more professional; the amount of sheer information poured out on what is going on has become almost too much to absorb. The true professionals in the Game—the professional portfolio managers— grow more skilled all the time. They are human and they make mistakes, but if you have your money managed by a truly alert mutual fund or even by one of the better banks, you will have a better job done for you than probably at any time in the past.
>
> But if you have your money managed for you, then you are not really interested, or at least the Game element—with that propensity to be paid for—does not attract you. I have known

a lot of investors who came to the market to make money, and they told themselves that what they wanted was the money: security, a trip around the world, a new sloop, a country estate, an art collection, a Caribbean house for cold winters. And they succeeded. So they sat on the dock of the Caribbean house, chatting with their art dealers and gazing fondly at the new sloop, and after a while it was a bit flat. Something was missing. If you are a successful Game player, it can be a fascinating, consuming, totally absorbing experience, in fact it has to be. If it is not totally absorbing, you are not likely to be among the most successful, because you are competing with those who do find it so absorbing.

But the real object of the Game is not money, it is the playing of the Game itself. For the true players, you could take all the trophies away and substitute plastic beads or whale's teeth, so long as there is a way to keep score, they will play.[10]

IF YOU'RE SO SMART, WHY AREN'T YOU RICH?

Can the individual investor, with limited time and resources, hope to succeed in a market full of professional investors and money managers? Surprisingly, many financial writers answer this question affirmatively.

We need to remember, as Humphrey B. Neill pointed out in *Tape Reading & Market Tactics*, that, regardless of age, gender, race, family background, level of education, degree of intellect, or station in life, every participant in the market shares one common trait: we are all human beings. Notwithstanding their financial education and market training, the professionals on Wall Street remain just as susceptible to human emotions and the contagion of the investment crowd as the first-time investor.

Adam Smith, in his book *The Money Game*, recounted John Maynard Keynes's description of the struggle between investment professionals as follows:

It might have been supposed that competition between expert professionals, possessing judgment and knowledge beyond that of the average private investor, would correct the vagaries of the ignorant individual left to himself. It happens, however, that the energies and skill of the professional investor and speculator are mainly occupied otherwise...They are concerned not with what an investment is really worth to a man who buys it "for keeps," but with what the market will value it at, under the influence of mass psychology, three months or a year hence.[11]

In his book *Irrational Exuberance*, Professor Robert J. Shiller wrote that there is little difference between professional and individual investors. His analysis was as follows:

Some observers believe that professional investment managers are more sensible and work to offset the **irrational exuberance** of the non-professional investing public. Therefore these observers might argue that a sharp distinction should be drawn between the behavior of the professionals and the nonprofessionals. Professional investors, however, are not immune from the effects of the popular investing culture that we observe in individual investors, and many of the factors described here no doubt influence their thinking as well. There is in fact no clear distinction between professional institutional investors and individual investors, since the professionals routinely give advice to the individual investors.[12] [Author's emphasis in **bold**.]

Peter Lynch wrote his best-selling book, *One Up on Wall Street,* in 1989 with noted financial writer John Rothchild. One of the most successful professional investors on Wall Street, Mr. Lynch told his readers that individual investors have an advantage over Wall Street professionals. He opened his book with the following: "This is where the author, a professional investor, promises the reader that for the next 300 pages he'll share the secrets of his success. But Rule number one, in my book, is: Stop listening to professionals! Twenty years in this business convinces me that any normal person using the customary three percent of the brain can pick stocks as well, if not better, than the average Wall Street expert."[13]

DO I NEED A HAIRCUT?

The answer to this question depends, to a certain extent, on who you ask. If you ask friends or family, you can probably expect an unbiased answer. If you ask your barber or hair stylist, you already know the answer. Now, let's rephrase the question. Ask your broker, "What should I do with my money?" Odds are he or she will tell you, "You should invest it." You can expect this answer regardless of the state of the market or the current economic cycle.

The broker is paid to facilitate investment purchases and sales, not give advice. Indeed, the broker hopes any advice given will lead to a transaction. In his amusing book, *Where Are the Customers' Yachts? or A Good Hard Look at Wall Street*, Fred Schwed, Jr. recounted the following story about an exchange between a broker and a customer in 1928:

> There was at that time engaged in the bank stock business, along with an awful lot of others, a large red-necked Texan. He had brought to his profession a booming Texas voice and a calcified conscience. On this occasion he had just sold a customer twenty shares of Guarantee Trust Company stock at $760 a share at the moment when it could have been purchased anywhere else at $730. The customer, the big sorehead, had just found this out and had called back with a view toward remonstrance. The Texan cut him short. "Suh," he boomed, "you-all don't appreciate what

the policy of this firm is. This-heah firm selects investments foh its clients not on a basis of Price, but of Value!"[14]

John Rothchild is a business writer who, in 1985, took a year off from work to learn everything he could about investments and Wall Street. He chronicled the year in his book, *A Fool and His Money, The Odyssey of an Average Investor*. He investigated what it takes to become a stockbroker. He learned that, at that time, it took approximately four months to become a licensed stockbroker. A licensed beauty parlor operator needed six months of training, and earning a plumber's license required two years of study. Rothchild attended broker-training sessions at major brokerage firms. He discovered that the majority of the training was devoted to sales techniques. He concluded his exposition of the classes with the following observation: "There were hour-long classes in various aspects of stocks and bonds that I would have mentioned earlier, except inserting them as an afterthought gives you a better idea of their relative importance as against, say, sales."[15]

It seems to me that an individual who researches investment opportunities and chooses the one that meets his or her requirements does not really need a broker's advice. Indeed, an individual investor with an investment strategy who is willing to do some research may be better off without help.

HOPE IS NOT A PLAN

Many stock purchases are based on psychological, not financial, factors. In his book *A Random Walk Down Wall Street*, Professor Burton Malkiel pointed out, "Stocks are bought on expectations—not on facts."[16]

In his book *When to Sell—Inside Strategies for Stock-Market Profits*, Justin Mamis discussed expectations as follows:

Stocks are bought not in fear but in hope. No matter what the stock did in the past, it assumes a new life once a purchaser owns it, and he looks forward to a rosy future—after all, that's why he singled it out in the first place. But these simple expectations become complicated by what actually happens. The stock acquires a new past, beginning from the moment of purchase, and with that past come doubts, new concerns, new conflicts. The purchaser's stock portfolio quickly becomes a portfolio of psychic dilemmas, with ego, id, superego, and reality in a state of constant battle…especially since, in the stock market, one is never quite sure what the reality is.

Let's be straightforward about it: the widespread and deep-rooted neuroses that affect virtually all decisions in the stock market are the subject for a different kind of analysis. Stock-market analysis is **the task of separating real possibilities from mere hopes**. And the path to doing this successfully is by concentrating on what you **do** know because it is actually happening—current prices, volume, statistics, etc.—rather than on what might happen or should happen.[17] [Author's emphasis in **bold**.]

In his book *The Battle for Investment Survival*, Gerald Loeb wrote, "Market values are fixed only in part by balance sheets and income statements; much more by the hopes and fears of humanity; by greed, ambition, acts of God, invention, financial stress and strain, weather, discovery, fashion and numberless other causes impossible to be listed without omission."[18]

Every individual, whether investing for the long term or speculating for a quick profit, must recognize the emotional forces that prey upon him or her. One of the best ways to reduce the emotional aspects of stock ownership is to remember Adam Smith's advice:

You can see that all this is leading to another of Smith's Irregular Rules, this one that the identity of the investor and that of the investing action must be coldly separate. A stock is, for all practical purposes, a piece of paper that sits in a bank vault. Most likely you will never see it. It may or may not have an Intrinsic Value, what it is worth on any given day depends on the confluence of buyers and sellers that day. The most important thing to realize is simple: The stock doesn't know you own it. All those marvelous things, or those terrible things, that you feel about a stock, or a list of stocks, or an amount of money represented by a list of stocks, all of those things are unreciprocated by the stock or group of stocks. You can be in love if you want to, but that piece of paper doesn't love you, and unreciprocated love can turn into masochism, narcissism, or, even worse, market losses and unreciprocated hate.[19]

WORD OF MOUTH

Humans have been communicating since they first started drawing pictures on cave walls. Robert J. Shiller, in his excellent book *Irrational Exuberance*, wrote about the innate human trait of information sharing, especially in person-to-person exchanges: "The human mind is the product of evolution almost entirely in the absence of the printed word, e-mail, the Internet, or any other artificial means of communication… The incessant exchange of information is a fundamental characteristic of our species."[20]

Human communication is basically the sharing of information. Any time two or more people meet, they communicate. In light of the inherent uncertainty in the market, individual investors are always looking for something or somebody to help reduce investment risk. You must remember that any such information, regardless of how it's presented, can be only one of three things: fact, rumor, or opinion.

As human beings we strive to learn things in order to reduce life's uncertainty. As investors, however, we must resist the urge to act upon one form of communication: the stock tip. Investors need to go slow when presented with tips. Facts and rumors can be checked out. Third-party opinion is just that, which makes it no better than an investor's personal analysis of a situation. Opinions differ, and, as they say, that's what makes for a horse race. The investor must weigh anyone else's opinion against his or her own information. If the tip is truly insider information, acting on it is illegal.

If someone should offer you an inside tip, please remember Philip Carret's advice in his book *The Art of Speculation* and consider yourself the thousandth rather than the first or second person to get the story.

COGITO, ERGO SUM—INVESTORS CONCLUDED

The Latin quote in the title—*cogito, ergo sum*—is usually translated as "I think, therefore I am" and is attributed to the French philosopher Rene Descartes. It originally appeared, in French, in 1637 in his work *Discourse on the Method* and again, in Latin, in his 1644 *Principles of Philosophy*.

While it may work in philosophy studies, it can actually be a trap when dealing with investments. Just because you think you are investing, it does not automatically make you an investor. You need to step back and really think about what you are doing and, more importantly, why. In short you need a strategy to guide your investments.

As we have seen in chapter three, when you start to think about investing, leave your emotions at the door and remain dispassionate. Never forget Adam Smith's rule: "The stock doesn't know you own it."[21]

We will explore various investment strategies in the next chapters.

4

Investment Strategies:
Fundamental Analysis

GOLD MINING, HANG GLIDING, AND RANDOM WALKING

You can roughly divide investment strategies into three overall types: fundamental analysis, technical analysis, and the random walk theory, more technically known as the efficient market hypothesis. A majority of fundamental investors study the financial data and prospects of companies to decide whose stock to buy. Most technical investors pay attention to price levels and trading volume either of the market in general or of a particular stock in an effort to determine the probable direction in which either or both of them might be headed. Proponents of the efficient market hypothesis reject the other two. In fact they do not believe fruitful analysis of any type is possible. They believe a stock's price says it all, and all market moves are random.

Those folks who make investments based on fundamental analysis, the gold miners, look for public companies with financial characteristics they feel will lead to an investment profit. They analyze things like the company's price earnings ratio, debt to equity level, asset to liability ratio, revenue and earnings growth rates, return on assets or on equity, profit margins, dividend payout ratios, interest coverage ratios, quality of management, overall prospects of the general industry in which the company does business, and the like. They are searching for gold nuggets in a mine full of financial data.

People who look to technical analysis, the hang gliders, look at either the state of the market in general and the way its overall price level is acting or a particular stock and its price movement. They pay attention to the price action of a stock, not its financial characteristics. They analyze things like sixty-five and two-hundred-day average price movements, trading volumes, advances and declines in prices, prices being stalled at or breaking through resistance levels, price charts, and the like. They want to catch the prevailing wind and ride it to a profit.

Economists in business schools developed the efficient market hypothesis. They believe that markets constantly and efficiently set the price for each and every stock in the market. Since the market price reflects everything known about a stock at the time, proponents of the random walk theory do not think fundamental or technical analysis will provide an investor with any benefit or advantage.

Each form of investing has its proponents and detractors. The following individuals are famous gold miners.

PHILIP CARRET

Philip L. Carret was one of the early practitioners of value investing, one of the forms of fundamental analysis. He wrote a series of articles for *Barron's*, a weekly financial publication, in 1926. Those articles became the book *The Art of Speculation*, first published in 1930. At the time he wrote his articles in 1926, the term *speculation* had some of the same negative connotations that still exist today. This is what he had to say:

What, after all, is speculation? The redoubtable Webster gives a number of definitions. Among them we find (1) "mental view of anything in its various aspects; intellectual examination"; (2) "the act or practice of buying land or goods, etc., in expectation of the rise of price and of selling them at an advance." To the second he added the complacent observation that "a few men have been enriched but many have been ruined by speculation." According to Webster, the motive is the test by which we must distinguish between an investment and a speculative transaction. The man who bought United States Steel at 60 in 1915 in anticipation of selling at a profit is a speculator according to Webster, though he may have changed his mind about selling and added the stock to his list of permanent investments. On the other hand, the gentleman who bought American Telephone at 95 in 1921 to enjoy the dividend return of better than 8% is an investor, though he may have succumbed to the temptation of a 10-point profit a few weeks later. Although the outcome of the transaction may contradict the original intention of the party chiefly interested, it is obviously impossible to omit the factor of motive in defining speculation.

Perhaps the best sort of speculation, and the kind that is most likely to be successful, is that which regards it as the business management of a fund. What does the manager of a business do? He controls men, materials and money, seeking to handle them in such a way that the business will produce a profit. Conceiving the speculator as manager of a business it will be seen that he also controls men, materials and money. The money is the starting point of his business, the materials are the securities which he buys and sells, the men are the directors and managers of the companies in whose securities he invests.[1]

CARRET'S INVESTMENT PRECEPTS

Mr. Carret listed his precepts for fundamental value investing as follows:

1. *Never hold fewer than ten different securities covering five different fields of business.*

   This provides a minimum amount of diversification—the old rule against keeping all of your eggs in one basket.

2. *At least once in six months reappraise every security held.*

   Mr. Carret suggests you look at each stock in your portfolio and ask whether you would buy the same stock for the same price it is selling at today. The price you paid for the stock is irrelevant in this exercise. You are looking at the investment anew. He recommends that if your answer would be no, then sell it and reinvest the proceeds.

3. *Keep at least half the total fund in income-producing securities.*

   At the time Mr. Carret wrote this, income-producing securities, corporate or government bonds paying interest, were considered a higher grade of investment than common stocks that did not pay any dividends. The risk of loss was considered significantly smaller. The investment quality of the bonds was the attraction, not the income itself.

4. *Consider yield the least important factor in analyzing any stock.*

   Mr. Carret explained that the speculative investor is mainly interested in an increase in the market value of the stock he or she purchases. The dividend income is not the goal. If the investor needs income from the funds, Mr. Carret considered that a sign the investor could not afford to speculate in the first place.

5. *Be quick to take losses, reluctant to take profits.*

The underlying assumption for his statement is that the investor is looking for a long-term increase in the value of his or her investment portfolio, not quick trading profits.

6. *Never put more than 25% of a given fund into securities about which detailed information is not readily and regularly available.*

In the 1920s, before there were federal securities regulations, there were few if any requirements that public companies provide financial information about their businesses to the public. Only the large shareholders, directors, and officers knew what was really going on. The individual investor back then had to work hard to learn much of anything about the state of affairs of the companies in which he or she had invested. Such is not the case today. If you can't easily and readily learn about a company's business operations and results on a regular basis, you probably should not invest in its stock.

7. *Avoid "inside information" as you would the plague.*

Looking at the psychological aspects of tips, Mr. Carret said they appeal to an investor's vanity, since such confidential news sets the recipient apart from the rest of the market. As mentioned earlier, he recommended that the person view himself or herself as being the thousandth rather than the first or second to get the story. Such lack of self-pride would, in Mr. Carret's words, be "well rewarded."

8. *Seek facts diligently, advice never.*

Mr. Carret told the story of a gentleman who was offered the chance to purchase a significant (one-sixth) interest in a new technology company of the time, American Telephone & Telegraph, for $10,000. He sought the advice of a friend in a similar industry, the president of Western Union Telegraph Co., who advised him to save his money. His friend viewed the new invention, the telephone, as impracticable. And, as they say, the rest is history.

9. *Ignore mechanical formulas for valuing securities.*

Although Mr. Carret recognized that some measures of a company are helpful, he warned against "unintelligent use of a convenient yardstick of values." He gave the example of the price earnings ratio, which is calculated by dividing a stock price by the prior twelve months' per-share earnings. The result represents the price earnings ratio. The higher it is, the more expensive the stock appears to be. Mr. Carret said this ratio is a good start, but the investor cannot rely on it alone. Intelligent analysis will always come down to careful consideration of all aspects of both a company and its stock.

10. *When stocks are high, money rates rising, business prosperous, at least half a given fund should be placed in short-term bonds.*

This rule recognizes the cyclical nature of the stock market. Mr. Carret was suggesting that when a market top appears likely, the cautious investor should sell his or her stock and put the proceeds into income-producing securities to wait out the imminent and inevitable fall in prices.

11. *Borrow money sparingly and only when stocks are low, money rates low or falling, and business depressed.*[2]

When Mr. Carret wrote the articles that became his book, many individual investors bought their stocks on margin, which means they put up only a small portion of the purchase price and borrowed the balance from the brokerage house that sold them the stock. The problem was that if the stock went down enough to wipe out the small equity held by the investor, the loan was called, and the investor would be sold out of the stock by the broker to recoup the loan, resulting in a loss of the entire investment. He is recommending that an investor should borrow on a limited scale and only when the stock market is in the doldrums.

DON CORLEONE, JAMES BROWN, AND BENJAMIN GRAHAM

Don Corleone was the original Godfather, the head of a New York Mafia family, in Mario Puzo's 1969 best-selling book of the same name. James Brown, the iconic singer, was known as the Godfather of Soul. Benjamin Graham could rightfully claim the title of godfather of value investing, the core of fundamental stock analysis.

Mr. Graham coauthored the 1934 textbook *Security Analysis* with David Dodd. The book he is best remembered for, *The Intelligent Investor*, was published for individual investors in 1949. He revised the book four times, with the last edition published in 1973. The book is still in print today.

Like Philip Carret, Ben Graham believed that the best approach for an investor was to view his or her stock portfolio as a business and to purchase stocks in a businesslike manner. He advised the individual investor to ignore the fluctuations of the market and to value a stock strictly on the financial condition of the company.

Mr. Graham likened the market to a voting machine in which investors cast their cash ballots for the most popular investment candidates. He felt that ultimately the market becomes a weighing machine—that is, a scale measuring the economic weight, or value, of stocks and setting prices accordingly. He advised investors to find the stocks with market prices below the financial worth, or intrinsic value, of the companies they represent. He thought individual investors should buy undervalued stocks and wait for the market to accurately weigh them. At that point the market would bid the company's stock price up, resulting in a profit.

By finding companies worth more than their market prices by significant amounts, the investor could enjoy Graham's "margin of safety,"
thereby avoiding substantial losses. Ben Graham recommended viewing
a stock not as a market bet but rather as a minority ownership in a business. The price paid for that ownership, if too high, would never lead
to a profit because the business could not ultimately justify the amount
paid. The true investment value of the stock is based on how much the
investor pays for it at the time of purchase. The price paid for a security
today does indeed determine the profit to be made tomorrow.

Ben Graham contrasted what he felt was an investment with what
he termed *speculation*. A safe investment requires thorough analysis of a
company. The investor is looking for safety of principal and an adequate
return. In other words, find a company whose stock will, in all probability, not result in a loss. He was very strict about this definition, saying that anything else was mere speculation.

Mr. Graham advised an asset allocation between high-quality bonds
and common stock, with a percentage of bonds neither below 25 percent nor above 75 percent of the portfolio. Common stocks make up
the difference. Graham felt that the easiest allocation was 50 percent
in bonds and 50 percent in stocks. He recommended that if the percentages between the two investment categories changed due to market
movements by as much as 5 percent, it was time to rebalance the portfolio by selling bonds and buying stocks or vice versa in order to retain
the desired percentages. In effect this is a very easy form of market timing; however, it's emotionally difficult to do. If the stock component of
the portfolio has appreciated to such an extent that the portfolio is out
of balance, the individual investor will find it hard to sell some of the
gainers and leave the party.

Like Philip Carret, Benjamin Graham recommended a diversified
stock portfolio. He suggested a portfolio with a minimum of ten and a
maximum of thirty different companies. Investors should consider only

"large, prominent and conservatively financed" companies. He admitted this description was indefinite, but he believed that it provided a general sense of what he was looking for. His type of company would have a continuous record of paying dividends for not less than ten years. As a general rule, Mr. Graham looked for a stock with a price/earnings ratio no higher than twenty times the company's last twelve months' earnings and not exceeding fifteen times its average earnings for the past three years.

To put it bluntly, Ben Graham wanted to buy stocks on the cheap. He looked for companies undervalued by the market. A quick measure of this is the price/earnings (P/E) ratio, which is the market price of the stock divided by the earnings per share (usually for the prior four quarters). This ratio shows what investors in the market are willing to pay for each one dollar of company earnings. The lower the ratio; the cheaper the stock. Another way to look at the P/E ratio is to think of it in years. If the company earned two dollars per share in the trailing twelve-month period and the price is thirty dollars per share (P/E of fifteen), it will take fifteen years for the company to earn the price of the share if per-share earnings remain at two dollars. Remember, this is earnings, not dividends.

Graham also looked at the converse of the P/E ratio—the earnings/price ratio. He recommended the investor look for a company with an earnings/price ratio equal to or greater than the prevailing interest rate for high grade (AA or better) corporate bonds. This comparison of the earnings/price ratio to the interest rate of high-quality corporate bonds actually served to establish the P/E ratio he was looking for in a company. As an example, let's assume that the prevailing interest rate for bonds rated AA or above is 6 percent. He recommended looking for a company with a P/E ratio that was the converse of 6 percent—a P/E ratio of seventeen (one hundred divided by six). Although it's simple math, he felt this calculation could protect the investor from making expensive purchase mistakes.

In addition to investing based on these ratios, Mr. Graham recommended companies with the following additional financial benchmarks: (i) **current assets** that exceeded **current liabilities** by 150 percent; (ii) debt of not more than 110 percent of current assets; (iii) earnings that were growing for each of the last five years (no losses in any year); (iv) a record of increasing dividends over a good number of years; and (v) a price that was less than 120 percent of the **net tangible assets**.

The bolded terms above may be unfamiliar to new investors. Many accounting terms are clearly explained by Ben Graham and Spencer B. Meredith in their book *The Interpretation of Financial Statements*, which was published in 1937. **Current assets** are defined as cash, cash equivalents (assets immediately convertible into cash), receivables due within one year, and inventories. Inventories, for a manufacturing concern, would include raw materials, goods in process of manufacture, and finished goods. Sometimes packing and shipping supplies are included. These assets are usually stated at the lower of cost or market value. **Current liabilities** are claims payable to third parties within one year. **Tangible assets** are all physical and financial assets, such as factories, inventory, cash, accounts receivable, and investments. **Intangible assets** include items such as goodwill and intellectual property, such as patents, trademarks, and the like. Although trademarks and patents obviously help generate a company's earnings (think of the words *Coca-Cola* in their distinctive script), it is hard to establish a value for them. Mr. Graham usually excluded them from his valuation of assets when analyzing a company. He defined **net tangible assets** as a company's tangible assets less all of the company's liabilities. He included both current and long-term debts.

An individual who intends to invest in common stocks and does not have an accounting background should get a copy of Graham's *The Interpretation of Financial Statements*. An investor with accounting training will benefit from this book as well since it focuses on the aspects of financial statements which are most important to an investor. A hardcover version of the 1937 edition was republished by HarperCollins Publishers in 1998, with an introduction by Michael Price. It is not a dry textbook but rather a short lesson in accounting for investors, clearly written.

AL FRANK

Al Frank wrote an investment letter, *The Prudent Speculator*, for many years. He put his investment advice together into a book, *The Prudent Speculator: Al Frank on Investing*, published in 1989. He updated it in 1996 in a new edition titled *Al Frank's New Prudent Speculator*. Mr. Frank started his updated edition by posing the question that bedevils every beginning investor—that is, how to choose an investment strategy.

Mr. Frank believed in value investing. He maintained that fundamental analysis was not that complicated and that any individual willing to take the time to learn it could master it. Wall Street perpetuates the myth that it takes advanced degrees, a genius IQ, and esoteric analysis of all sorts of business minutiae in order to succeed in the market. Frank maintained that you have learned everything necessary for successful investing by the sixth grade.

Mr. Frank listed several criteria he felt were good indicators of a corporation whose stock merited consideration. He suggested finding companies with a price to earnings ratio of less than ten times earnings with a return on equity (ROE) of 15 percent or better.

Al Frank stated there are actually two types of diversification the individual investor must keep in mind: stock diversification and time diversification. Mr. Frank recommended a stock portfolio with between twenty-five and thirty stocks in a minimum of fifteen different industries. He also counseled that no single stock should exceed 5 percent of the portfolio's total value.

Frank also discussed time diversification—in other words, how long an investor holds on to a stock. In these days of split-second trades generated with extremely fast computer programs, such an idea seems old fashioned. He wrote about a study published in the *Journal of Portfolio Management*, which measured the reduction of risk achieved by holding stocks for longer periods. The study concluded that the shorter the time you hold a stock, the more random its price movements may be, but over time this tends to even out. The longer a stock is held, the less risky the stock becomes. The term *risk* in this context means the degree of volatility in a stock's price movements. The volatility/risk of a stock diminishes the longer you hold it.

In order to hold a stock for a long time, the investor must have one very important trait: patience. He or she must be able to weather the ups and downs of the market—to resist the clamoring of Le Bon's crowd. Patience is only possible if the individual has confidence in his or her chosen investment strategy. Each investor must decide if a particular investment system makes sense (feels right) to him or her. Although the goals are entirely different, your investment strategy is similar, in one respect, to your religious beliefs. If you are not a true believer, you may not follow the religion's teachings when you must choose a course of behavior. If you do not have complete faith in the investing strategy you pick, you may not follow it when you are faced with Ben Graham's Mr. Market. Frank cited Warren Buffett's advice that if you would be driven to sell a stock that had declined by 50 percent, then you should not own common stocks. You must fully embrace your investment strategy to weather the storm without panicking.

WARREN BUFFETT

If there were a Mount Rushmore for investment greats, it would surely depict Warren Buffett's face. A student of Benjamin Graham, Mr. Buffett started out his investment career in Omaha, Nebraska, and, over fifty-plus years, shrewdly invested in stocks, bonds, and insurance companies. He made many of his early investors multimillionaires.

Mr. Buffett's company, Berkshire Hathaway, is the vehicle through which he makes his investments. It is publicly traded and could be viewed as a gigantic mutual fund run by one of the most successful fund managers in history. Ironically, the name of the company comes from one of his early investment mistakes, a New England textile manufacturer he liquidated after many years of financial struggle. He admits this investment was based, in large part, on his early investment style, the one he learned from Benjamin Graham—buying companies as cheaply as possible. Sometimes companies are cheap because they should be, not because the market has mistakenly undervalued them. These days Mr. Buffett says he looks for investments with an "attractive price."

Buffett recommended avoiding the groupthink so common on Wall Street by recounting a story from Mr. Graham:

Ben Graham told a story 40 years ago that illustrates why investment professionals behave as they do: An oil prospector moving to his heavenly reward, was met by St. Peter with bad news. "You're qualified for residence," said St. Peter, "but, as you can see, the compound reserved for oil men is packed. There's no way to squeeze you in." After thinking a moment, the prospector asked if he might say just four words to the present occupants. That seemed harmless to St. Peter, so the prospector cupped his hands and yelled, "Oil discovered in hell." Immediately the gate to the compound opened and all of the oil men marched out to head for the nether regions. Impressed, St. Peter invited the prospector to move in and make himself comfortable. The prospector paused. "No," he said, "I think I'll go along with the rest of the boys. There might be some truth to that rumor after all."[3]

The best way to learn Buffett's investing philosophy is to read his annual letters to the Berkshire Hathaway shareholders. All of them, starting in 1977, are available at the Berkshire Hathaway website. An easier way is to read *The Essays of Warren Buffett: Lessons for Corporate America*, an authorized compilation of material from the shareholder letters, edited by Lawrence A. Cunningham. The first edition was published in 2001, and a second edition came out in 2008.

CARRET, GRAHAM, FRANK, AND BUFFETT—A REPRISE

The collective careers of Philip Carret, Benjamin Graham, Al Frank, and Warren Buffet add up to around two hundred years in the stock market. The similarities among their respective investment strategies are striking. I will try to list some of those areas of consensus. A list of those financial attributes on which all four men agreed could be used by an individual investor as a basis for selecting stocks for his or her portfolio based on fundamental value principles.

All four of them invested in companies, not stocks. The first rule was that any investment analysis be conducted in a businesslike manner. They each ignored what the market crowd said about a stock. They wanted to understand a company's business—the product or service the company provided to its customers and its financial condition. As Warren Buffett told his shareholders, he approached an investment in a publicly traded stock as if he were going to buy the entire company. Carret, Graham, and Frank all started their individual stock analyses in much the same way.

Carret, Graham, and Frank discussed asset allocation—that is, the division of an investment portfolio between equities and bonds. In general they all recommended approximately a fifty/fifty split between stocks and bonds. I have always liked the age-related method of allocating the bonds and stocks in an individual investor's portfolio. The investor subtracts his or her age from one hundred. The percentage of your portfolio in bonds would be your age, and the percentage in stocks would be the difference. This form of asset allocation seems a little better tailored to the individual and his or her stage in life. Young investors have ample time to recover from market losses, so their portfolios can contain a larger percentage of equities. Older investors, sadly, do not. A retired investor might safeguard his or her portfolio from market gyrations with a larger percentage of interest-bearing instruments. Those could be high-grade corporate bonds or US Treasuries, both of short duration.

Three of the four men also recommended diversification. Buffett takes the counter position, suggesting that an investor concentrate his or her purchases in a small number of stocks. Carret, Graham, and Frank recommended diversification with ownership in ten to thirty different stocks in a wide range of industries. Mr. Frank maintained that no company should represent more than 5 percent of the total value of an individual's holdings. Although differing on stock diversification, Buffett agrees with Al Frank on time diversification—that is, longer holding periods reduce overall market risk. Warren Buffett told his Berkshire Hathaway shareholders that his preferred holding time for an investment was somewhere close to "forever."

Another metric they all mentioned is a stock's price/earnings ratio. A company's P/E is very much like the price per pound for meat. A stock selling for eighty dollars per share with a P/E of ten is cheaper than a stock selling for forty dollars per share with a P/E of fifteen. The actual price for a dollar of earnings is one of the easiest ways to measure what an investor is actually paying for shares. Warren Buffett looks at a company's P/E to see if the company has an "attractive price." Just like the price per pound, a P/E reflects how expensive the stock is. Everyone agrees that the lower the P/E the better. However, an individual investor cannot pick just stocks with low P/Es, since in some instances the market may have correctly evaluated the company as a bad investment, with a resulting low P/E ratio.

The four gentlemen also felt a company's return on equity was an important measure of its financial strength. The higher the ROE number, the better the job the company's management is doing for the shareholders. ROE is the ratio of the annual earnings of a company divided by its equity. Al Frank suggested that a 15 percent ROE was a sign of a potentially good investment. However, there is one trap in this metric. An individual investor should look for a company with a high ROE whose debt is not excessive. If the equity percentage of the total capitalization of a company is only 10 percent and the remaining 90 percent is debt, it would not be hard to have a high ROE. The equity percentage is very small, and the company could be viewed as overleveraged. A company worth considering as an investment should have a high ROE (15 to 20 percent or better) based on a significant equity base with moderate debt (debt that is no more than 30 to 40 percent of a company's total capitalization).

Other than Buffett, they all recommended the individual investor also look for companies with histories of dividend payments (even better if the dividends have been regularly increased) and histories of increasing earnings. By *histories* they meant at least the last five years. As mentioned above, another sign of a well-managed company is one with a moderate amount of debt when compared to the company's total capitalization. This means the earnings of the company can be directed toward increasing the business and paying dividends, not paying interest to lenders. A certain amount of debt is to be expected, but if the company is heavily indebted (significantly more debt than equity), this could presage financial problems for the company during difficult economic times. Given traditional economic cycles, the individual investor must expect some periods of economic stress during his or her investment career. It is during a down economy, or recession, when truly strong business managers excel and keep their companies on track.

We have now devoted quite a bit of time to learning about value investing, one form of fundamental analysis, from four highly regarded value investors. There are two additional types of fundamental analysis: growth investing and contrarian investing.

GROWTH INVESTING—PHILIP A. FISHER

In one of his shareholder letters, Warren Buffett told his readers that the terms *value investing* and *growth investing* are the same. He felt that a value investor should be looking for companies whose business prospects and profits appear to be on an ascending trajectory for the foreseeable future. Investing in growth stocks with revenues and earnings growing at a pace exceeding that of the general market is a well-respected investment philosophy. A famous proponent of growth investing was Philip A. Fisher, who wrote his classic *Common Stocks and Uncommon Profits* in 1958. He looked for companies that devoted a large portion of their earnings to research and development of new products. He was also a long-term investor. It is reported that Mr. Fisher invested in Motorola in 1955 and held the stock until his death in 2004.

Philip Fisher listed fifteen attributes to look for in a promising stock. He indicated that a company should offer products with a potential market large enough to provide significant sales increases while generating a significant profit margin. In addition the company had to be able to improve on its products through continuous research and development in order to be ready to sell new models (in today's parlance, version 2.0) when current models had run their life cycles. The company must also be developing completely new products.

In addition to these financial and product characteristics, Mr. Fisher was interested in a company's labor relations, the depth of its management bench, its executive development program, and the quality of its expense controls. He looked for companies capable of financing growth with earnings or debt in order to avoid stock dilution and maintain his stock position. If an investor owns one hundred shares of a company with one thousand issued and outstanding shares, he or she has a 10 percent interest in the company. If that company issues an additional one thousand shares and the shareholder does not buy any, then that one-hundred-share percentage drops from 10 to 5 percent.

The company's management was also important to Mr. Fisher. He wanted to find companies with honest management interested in the long-term success of the companies, not just their next quarterly results. He explained this as follows:

> Furthermore, the companies into which the investor should be buying if greatest gains are to occur are companies which over the years will constantly, through the efforts of technical research, be trying to produce and sell new products and new processes. By the law of averages, some of these are bound to be costly failures…How a management reacts to such matters can be a valuable clue to the investor. The management that does not report as freely when things are going badly as when they are going well usually "clams up" in this way for one of several rather significant reasons. It may not have a program worked out to solve the unanticipated difficulty. It may have become panicky. It may not have an adequate sense of responsibility to its stockholders seeing no reason why it should report more than what may seem expedient at the moment. In any event, the investor will do well to exclude from investment any company that withholds or tries to hide bad news.[4]

YOU GOTTA GO WHERE THEY AIN'T

You get in your car to go to work and turn on the radio. The radio announcer reports that the expressway you use every day is totally bogged down, and traffic is at a crawl because of a multivehicle accident. Do you follow your usual pattern and drive to the on-ramp? Obviously not. You take an alternate route to avoid the traffic jam; you avoid the crowd. Many of the authors we have discussed advise against joining investment crowds. Some investors take an additional step. They not only try to avoid being sucked into the emotions of the market crowd; they intentionally head in the opposite direction. These are the contrarian investors.

Most parents can remember their children's "terrible twos." As a two-year-old takes those first steps toward independence, the little tyke will repeatedly resist parental commands. "No" becomes his or her mantra. Over the years countless mothers have looked at their little rebels and said, "You are so contrary."

Humphrey B. Neill, known as The Vermont Ruminator, wrote *The Art of Contrary Thinking* in 1954. His opening line in the book is "When everyone thinks alike, everyone is likely to be wrong." He counseled his readers to avoid the crowd mentality that rules Wall Street, citing Gustave Le Bon's book *The Crowd*.

However, Mr. Neill did not think that the crowd was always wrong. He had the following to say about the investing public:

> Is the public always wrong? This is probably the most frequently asked question about the Theory of Contrary Opinion. For a correct answer we need to change the words in this question. Let me put it this way: Is the public wrong **all the time**? The answer is decidedly, "No." The public is perhaps right more of the time than not. In stock market parlance, the public is right **during** the trends but wrong at both ends. One can assert that

the public is usually wrong at junctures of events and at terminals of trends. So, to be cynical, you might say, "Yes, the public is always wrong when **it pays to be right**—but is far from wrong in the meantime."[5] [Author's emphasis in **bold**.]

Neill noted that no investor, including the contrarian, can accurately forecast such junctures of events or terminals of trends. The contrarian, sensing the ongoing rush of crowd emotion, will usually find himself or herself leaving the market party early. The departure may be weeks or even months ahead of the game-changing event or end of the trend, but it is better to be safe than sorry. Like Cinderella, many investors remain at the ball well past midnight and rue that stay the morning after. Neill believed this to be simply human nature, which he described as follows: "It has been my observation over a long period that it takes us average humans a considerable interval to shift our viewpoints, once we have established a given mental outlook. That is, if we have (mentally) accepted a trend as moving in one direction, we are not inclined to change our outlook **until well after the trend turns**"[6] (Author's emphasis in **bold**).

CONTRARIAN INVESTING—DAVID DREMAN
Many consider David Dreman one of the foremost contrarian investors. His book, *The New Contrarian Investment Strategy*, published in 1982, explored the psychological underpinnings of investment decisions. He rejected the idea of an efficient market in which investors always act rationally. Today there is an entire field of study called behavioral economics that researches how an individual's psychological makeup can affect and control his or her investment decisions. Mr. Dreman recounted the results of several psychological experiments that revealed how people approach risk and potential loss. Some of the research also dealt with the effects groupthink can have on an investor's decisions.

Dreman wrote that the hallmark of a contrarian is his or her search for stocks with low price to earnings ratios. A low P/E relative to the overall market is an indication that the investing public either is unaware of the company or is intentionally shunning it. This could be because of a general lack of interest in the company (it's not seen as a hot stock) or because of a perceived economic weakness in the company or its industry. Put simply, a low P/E stock is not popular; it is out of favor with the Wall Street community. Contrarians look for these stocks, relying on the rule of regression to the mean. Sooner or later Wall Street will recognize the financial value of the stock and start to bid up its price as the company or its results finally garner investor attention. This is akin to Ben Graham's idea that the market starts as a voting machine for a stock, but sooner or later it becomes a scale, weighing value.

One of my favorite stories from Dreman's book is about a mutual fund company, Bull and Bear, Inc. The fund managers decided to cater to both types of investors at a time of market indecision. They established two mutual funds—a bull fund for investors who thought the market was going to go up and a bear fund for those who thought the market was going to decline. He reported, "Both lost money! That year, the bull fund declined 15 percent and the bear fund 9 percent."[7]

Dreman listed his rules for the contrarian investor. He agreed with Messrs. Carret, Graham, Frank, and Buffet that a company had to have a strong economic position with acceptable financial ratios. He also agreed with Mr. Fisher that a company should demonstrate a rate of earnings growth that exceeds the average earnings growth rate of the market. He looked for companies with histories of increasing dividends over time. He also believed in diversification (equal investments in fifteen to twenty different stocks ranging over ten to twelve industries).

Although each of the previously mentioned authors recommended not overpaying for a stock, Mr. Dreman made a stock's P/E ratio the centerpiece of his investment philosophy. His primary rule was to buy low P/E stocks listed on the New York Stock Exchange. He told his readers, "In my own application of the low P/E approach, I have used the bottom 40 percent of stocks according to P/E's for stock selection."[8] Like Ben Graham, David Dreman was always looking for a cheap stock, as measured by its P/E ratio. By limiting his purchases to the NYSE, he concentrated on mid- to large-sized companies.

PETER LYNCH—FINDING INVESTMENTS AT HOME

Like Philip Fisher, Peter Lynch was a growth investor. As the portfolio manager for the Fidelity Magellan mutual fund from May 1977 to May 1990, he posted market-leading returns for his fund investors year after year. Peter Lynch wrote his best-selling book, *One Up On Wall Street*, in 1989 with noted financial writer John Rothchild.

In a conversational manner, Mr. Lynch wrote about the highs and lows of his career and explained why and how the individual investor can beat the annual returns of professional investors. He advised his readers to look around and find the companies whose products or services are routinely used at home. His best example was L'eggs. I do not know if they are still being sold, but L'eggs was a brand of panty hose packaged in plastic eggs and displayed on racks in grocery stores in the 1970s. Mr. Lynch explained that the manufacturer of L'eggs realized that women went to department stores to buy their nylons only once every six weeks. However, these same women went to the grocery store usually twice a week. L'eggs remains one of the most successful products of its era. Mr. Lynch pointed out that he did not discover this investment opportunity; his wife did. She told him about the product, and he found out that Hanes was the company that had come up with this unique selling concept. He did his research and discovered that the company was financially solid. His investment in Hanes stock turned into a "sixbagger"—Mr. Lynch's term for a stock whose value increased sixfold. Lynch's advice is to think about a good product or service you use in your life. Identify the manufacturer or service provider and research the company if it is publicly traded. If the company meets your fundamental investment requirements, buy the stock.

I know of an individual who had a bout with cancer several years ago, which, fortunately, was very treatable. His doctor recommended daily radiation treatments for a couple of weeks. Every day he climbed up on a table and was run through the radiation machine. He noticed the brand of machine, checked out the company, and bought some of its stock. This story has a happy ending. Both he and the company's stock are doing fine more than ten years on.

Please forgive me for recounting another story along these lines, but I can't resist. While picking up, for what seemed the hundredth time, worn-out and broken crayons from his daughter's latest art project, a friend of mine found an investment. Crayons had been made by Binney & Smith, Inc. since 1903, and the company was publicly traded. He researched its financials, which were good, and bought some of the stock. When Binney & Smith was purchased by Hallmark in 1984, he netted a sizable gain—enough to keep his daughter in crayons for a lifetime. Keep your eyes open. There may be a good investment lying at your feet.

FUNDAMENTAL ANALYSIS—THE GOLD MINERS

If you consider the common financial characteristics mentioned by each of the proponents of fundamental analysis we have met, you can probably come up with a fundamental formula for your own investment strategy. Here are some of their consensus ideas:

1. Buy companies, not stocks. Investing should be conducted in a businesslike manner based on financial facts, not emotion. Peter Lynch suggested looking around your house for products made by companies you might consider.

2. Diversify. Each author suggested investing in a number of companies. Al Frank recommended that no one stock should account for more than 5 percent of an investor's total equity portfolio. Mathematically this means that a well-rounded portfolio would hold at least twenty stocks in different industries.

3. Earnings and dividend growth. Everyone recommended companies with histories of at least three and, preferably, five years of both earnings and dividend growth. Philip Fisher looked for companies with earnings that exceeded the market's overall earnings growth. When looking at dividends, the investor must also check the payout ratio—that is, how much of each dollar of earnings is distributed to shareholders. A lower percentage indicates the dividend is safer than the dividend of a company that distributes a large percentage of its earnings to its owners. If the payout percentage is low, the company might not have to reduce the dividends if its earnings were to decline.

4. Low debt and high return on equity. When hard times hit, the company with a small percentage of debt in its capital structure has a better chance of weathering the downturn. Although the gold miners do not all agree on an acceptable level of debt, you get the sense that a company whose capital consisted of 70 percent equity and 30 percent debt would be one that these experts would consider a solid investment opportunity. A return on equity of 20 percent is considered a sign of a good company.

5. Avoid a high P/E ratio. The lower the P/E, the cheaper the stock based on its earnings. The P/E measures how much an investor is paying for each dollar of earnings. David Dreman pointed out that a high ratio is usually an indication that the market crowd has taken over, and the price is being bid up based on frenzy, not finances. Some companies might deserve a

low P/E due to poor performance or business prospects, so an investor cannot rely solely on this ratio.

6. Be patient and invest long term. All of the authors mentioned in this section recommended viewing investments as long-term commitments. Warren Buffett said his time line for holding a stock was "forever." Al Frank cited research that concluded that the volatility of the market is taken out of play if an investor holds his or her stocks for years, not weeks or months. He referred to this as *time diversification*. Each author also counseled patience. The individual investor should ignore market gyrations and stick with his or her personal investment strategy.

DR. BURTON MALKIEL'S RIPOSTE TO FUNDAMENTAL ANALYSIS

Proponents of the efficient market hypothesis, also called the random walk theory, reject, more or less, the fundamental and technical forms of analysis. I say "more or less" because there are three subsets of the random walk theory: the weak, semistrong, and strong forms. The essence of the theory is that the price of a stock, at any given moment, represents its true value, which varies in a random fashion as the stock is constantly repriced by the market.

One of the most famous of these random walkers is Professor Burton G. Malkiel, the Chemical Bank Chairman's professor of economics at Princeton University. His book, *A Random Walk Down Wall Street*, is the classic text on the efficient market hypothesis, first published in 1973. Professor Malkiel called fundamental analysis the "firm-foundation theory" of investing and described it as follows:

The firm-foundation theory argues that each investment instrument, be it a common stock or a piece of real estate, has a firm anchor of something called **intrinsic value**, which can be determined by careful analysis of present conditions and future prospects. When market prices fall below (rise above) this firm foundation of intrinsic value, a buying (selling) opportunity arises, because this fluctuation will eventually be corrected—or so the theory goes. Investing then becomes a dull but straightforward matter of comparing something's actual price with its firm foundation of value.[9] [Author's emphasis in **bold**.]

Professor Malkiel then points out its weaknesses as follows: "Despite its plausibility and scientific appearance, there are three potential flaws in this type of analysis. First, the information and analysis may be incorrect. Second, the security analyst's estimate of value may be faulty. Third, the market may not correct its 'mistake' and the stock price might not converge to its value estimate."[10]

Any investor drawn to fundamental analysis should keep Professor Malkiel's observations in mind. After reading this chapter, if fundamental analysis does not seem right to you, you may find technical analysis more appealing.

Investment Strategies: Technical Analysis

TECHNICAL ANALYSIS—HANG GLIDERS

I refer to technical investors as hang gliders, riding the winds of market sentiment, looking to profit from a stock's updraft or downdraft in price. Technical investors are often referred to as chartists since they graph the action of the market and/or individual stocks. They study their graphs of price movement and trading volume, looking for trends that reveal where market levels or an individual stock price might go (up or down) based on past performance. I think the technical form of investing could be said to rest on two principles: the economic law of supply and demand and a basic tenet of physics—the law of motion.

The law of supply and demand provides a model for analyzing what affects the price of an item in a market. If demand equals supply and buyers and sellers agree on price, the market is in balance, also called economic equilibrium. If such is not the case, the law of supply and demand states there are four possible outcomes, depending on existing circumstances in a market, for the price of anything for sale:

1. If demand for the item (number of buyers) increases and the supply of the item (number of items) remains unchanged, the price will rise.

2. If demand decreases and the supply is unchanged, the price will decrease.
3. If the supply increases and the demand remains unchanged, the price will decrease.
4. If the supply decreases and the demand is unchanged, the price will rise.

Keep in mind that these laws apply to each stock, so the market in general reflects the aggregate effects of the law of supply and demand on all of the individual stocks comprising the market.

I think technical analysis also borrows from one of the basic tenets of physics: Sir Issac Newton's first law of motion—a body at rest tends to stay at rest; a body in motion tends to stay in motion unless acted upon by an external force. Technical investors believe that a stock price, whether rising or falling, will continue in that direction until the price trend stops or changes direction from some outside force or event, which is called the point of inflection.

Charles H. Dow, the founder and first editor of *The Wall Street Journal*, wrote over two hundred editorials on the market. After Dow's death the editorials were organized into what was called the Dow theory. The theory holds that the market has three price movements or cycles. First is the "main movement," which may continue for anywhere from less than a year up to several years. This would be considered the major trend of the market. The next longest period is the "medium swing," which lasts from several days to up to three months within a main movement. It consists of any secondary or intermediate reaction to the main movement. The shortest period is the "short swing." These minor movements may continue from several hours up to a month or more. Many technical analysts believe that the Dow theory is the foundation of modern technical analysis. The difficulty is that all three movements can be roiling the market at the same time.

PRICE AND VOLUME MATTER

Technical investors map the market action of a stock. There is a book that is considered by many to be the Bible of technical analysis, much like *The Intelligent Investor* by Benjamin Graham is widely seen as the Bible of fundamental analysis. *Technical Analysis of Stock Trends*, coauthored in 1948 by Robert D. Edwards and John Magee, is seen as the best book on technical analysis. Its eighth and ninth editions are still in print today. Some consider the following excerpt from the book to be the all-time best description of technical analysis:

> The market price reflects not only the differing fears and guesses and moods, rational and irrational, of hundreds of potential buyers and sellers, but it also reflects their needs and resources—in total, factors which defy analysis and for which no statistics are obtainable. These are nevertheless all synthesized, weighted and finally expressed in the one precise figure at which a buyer and seller get together and make a deal. The resulting price is the only figure that counts.[1]

To me, this description bears a striking resemblance to the random walk theory.

Norman G. Fosback, a well-respected investment adviser and cofounder of The Institute of Econometric Research, wrote his enduring work, *Stock Market Logic, A Sophisticated Approach to Profits on Wall Street*, in 1976. The twenty-second edition was printed in 1993. In referring to a table of daily price/volume relationships for the period 1965 to 1972 depicted in his book, he wrote: "The most important conclusions to be gleaned from the table are: (1) rising price is a relatively bullish portent for future price changes and falling price is relatively bearish; (2) rising volume is even more bullish and falling volume is relatively bearish; (3) rising price accompanied by rising volume is the most bullish of all and falling price accompanied by falling volume is consistently bearish."[2]

Al Frank was a self-avowed value investor. However, he admitted he paid attention to technical analysis to improve the timing of his value investing. He discussed some of the technical investing tools he used in his book *Al Frank's New Prudent Speculator.*

If you look back at the advice of the value investors, you will see that for the most part they recommend investing for the long term. It seems to me that technical analysis focuses on a shorter time horizon. It appears to be more of a tool for speculation, looking for a profit within days, weeks or months—not a tool for investment in a stock you intend to hold for many years. However, some investors, like Justin Mamis, rely on technical analysis their entire careers and invest on the principle that there is a correlation between historical price and volume levels and future price movement.

THE TREND IS YOUR FRIEND—MOVING AVERAGES

Warren Buffett said that once he had purchased a stock, he could forget about the market and its gyrations. Al Frank pointed out that markets run in cycles of advance and decline in his classic, *Al Frank's New Prudent Speculator.*

When technical investors are poring over their charts, what are they looking for? There are many signs for the chartists to divine, but the overall trend of a stock or a market is one of the most popular. Studying moving averages is one of the basic exercises of the technical analyst. A moving average (M/A) provides the average price of a stock or a market over a set period. One of the most basic of these is the ten-day M/A for a stock.

We will create a ten-day M/A for an individual stock, since it is easily calculated. It helps to have graph paper on which you can create a vertical price line and a horizontal time line. Since you are calculating a number that is the average price of a stock over a given ten-day period, your graph will show only that one number (the average price) for the ten days going backward (the chosen time frame). For our example, you will keep track of a stock's price over ten consecutive days. When you have prices for ten days, add the prices up and divide by ten, which gives you your first average. Note that on your graph. Each day thereafter, you drop the stock price from eleven days ago and add in the latest price. You then recalculate the average for the new ten-day period and plot it on your graph. Over time, as you do your daily calculations and add the results to the graph, you will start to see one of three possible trends: up, down, or unchanged. Technical analysis holds that each of these trends can provide insight into where the stock price may head in the future.

Since you are creating your own chart, you can pick any time line for your average: five, ten, thirty, forty-five, sixty, or two hundred days or any other number of days of prices. It is a personal decision as to how many days to use in creating your M/A. Regardless of the number of days used, the exercise is the same. You drop the oldest price, add the newest, and average them. If you will be speculating over the long term, an M/A of two hundred days may be what you want. It would be of little value if you are trading on a daily basis, since it will not provide the immediacy you need. Conversely, if you intend to trade or speculate over an intermediate period (forty-five to sixty days), a ten-day M/A does not give you the longer-term chart your investment strategy may need.

I use the words *speculator* and *trader*, not *investor*, to describe technical analysts. This is intentional, since, as I said earlier, I believe technical analysis lends itself to short and intermediate holding periods. For the long-term, multiyear, value investor, such as Warren Buffett, market moves are not that important.

ADVANCES AND DECLINES—PORTRAIT OF A MARKET

If looking at one or more individual stocks, the technical analyst creates a chart of moving averages for each stock. If studying an entire market, the technical tool is the advance/decline line (A/D line).

The chartist using the A/D line gets the number of stocks advancing in price and the number of stocks declining in price for a trading day from the financial press. The next step is to net the advances against the declines to arrive at a number: positive if advances exceed declines and negative if the opposite occurs. If there were one thousand advances and seven hundred declines in a day (ignoring the number of unchanged stock prices) then the number to be added to the chart would be a positive three hundred.

Daily results alone are not looked upon as predictive since they will appear random. Graphing longer periods will show a trend or a point of inflection when the trend starts to reverse itself. Just as with moving averages, the chartist can choose his or her preferred period; five, ten, thirty, sixty, two hundred, or whatever other number of days seems appropriate to the individual. As with moving averages, the oldest number in the A/D line is dropped, and the newest number is added as each day passes.

Al Frank discussed some market rules about advances and declines in his book and pointed out that there can be all sorts of conflicting indications between the different periods, all of which are happening at the same time.

Mr. Frank's observations concerning conflicting A/D lines sum up the difficulties faced by a chartist. It would seem there is rarely, if ever, a clear signal as to what the market is going to do. No matter how many graphs the technical analyst creates, the individual must make the ultimate decision as to what they indicate. The interpretation of value by a fundamental analyst and the interpretation of indicators by a technical analyst are, essentially, different techniques to arrive at the same point. Regardless of the investment strategy employed, the individual must ultimately decide what to do with the information presented. As Justin Mamis said, "There is never enough information."[3]

SPEAKING VOLUMES

Moving averages and advance/decline lines show price movement, which is only half of the story. Technical analysts believe it is one thing to see which way prices are moving, but this does not give the full picture without the volume of the movement (number of shares traded). The price of a stock gives only the current value. Without the amount of stock traded, the price is of little informative worth. A hundred shares traded at twenty dollars is one thing; ten thousand shares traded at that price is quite a different story.

In addition to his book, *The Art of Contrary Thinking*, Humphrey B. Neill also wrote *Tape Reading & Market* Tactics, first published in 1931. It is still in print. In *Tape Reading* Neill explained the role of volume in technical analysis as follows:

For the sake of simplifying our problem, I shall here roughly define the three main types of volume-activity:

First: Increasing volume **during** an advance, with the intervening pauses or setbacks occurring on light volume. This is indicative of the underlying demand's being greater than the supply, and favors a resumption of the advance.

Second: Increased volume at the **top** of a rally, or of an advance, lasting for some time, with no appreciable gain in prices—an active churning of stock transactions without progress. This is indicative of a turning-point.

Third: A "tired," or struggling, advance, when stocks creep upward on light volume or "die" at the top. This indicates a lack of demand (few buying orders); and, whereas, selling-orders likewise are light, this action frequently marks a "rounding-over" turn, which may be followed by increased volume on the down side (when the sellers see that they cannot hope for much higher prices at the time). These struggling trends are subject to sudden reversals, particularly when they have endured for several days.

These types of action are present, but reversed in sequence, in declining markets.[4] [Author's emphasis in **bold**.]

Volume shows which way the money is flowing. Norman G. Fosback, in his work *Stock Market Logic, A Sophisticated Approach to Profits on Wall Street*, discussed several volume indicators he felt were important, including one he called on balance volume (OBV). Mr. Fosback explained that OBV is based on the theory that volume trends lead to price trends. In other words the volume of trading in a stock over a period presages the price of the stock, which will follow the volume either up or down.

CHARTING A COURSE

We have used the term *chartist* as another term for technical analyst. There are as many types of charts as there are chartists. The form of chart used is a personal decision that, I suspect, is dictated by the chart's presentation of information the technical analyst believes is both important and predictive. There are two popular charts used by many in the technical community: the bar chart (BC) and the point and figure chart (PF).

The BC, the most popular form of charting, gives the analyst a picture of price movement over time. The BC chartist notes the price points along the vertical axis and the discrete periods along the horizontal axis. The vertical line or bar within the graph shows the price movement for the selected time—a day, a week, a month, or any other period the chartist wants to work with. For our example, we'll use a daily bar. The top of the bar is the highest price of the stock that day. The bottom of the bar, conversely, is the lowest price of that day. The closing price within that price spread is noted with a horizontal hash or tick mark across the vertical bar. Creating a BC of daily prices takes time and patience because a few days of bars will not reveal much more than daily randomness—market noise, so to speak.

As we just learned, volume plays an important role in providing a complete picture. Many BC graphs will also indicate the volume for the selected period. In our example, the daily volume (again, as a vertical line) would be drawn below the price chart for each day. This is really a graph within a graph. If a stock trades several thousand shares a day, the volume chart can be set in thousands. If it trades only a few hundred shares daily then the volume can be set in hundreds. The goal in our example is to show the ebb and flow of both the stock's price movement and trading volume for each day.

The second most popular graph is the point and figure chart. The main difference between the BC and the PF chart forms is the fact that time is not an element in PF charts. The focus is solely on price movement up or down. The PF chartist designates a dollar value for each square on the graph: one dollar, five dollars, or any dollar amount he or she decides to use. The vertical axis on a PF chart lists prices. The horizontal axis on a PF chart does not have a value measure. So long as the price of a stock is advancing, the rise in price is indicated by Xs (each X representing the designated dollar box value) added in the same column. When the price goes into decline, the chartist moves to the next column to the right and notes the decline(s) with one or more Os starting at the first declining price point (again based on the dollar value of each box). Additional Os are added in that same column so long as the price continues to decline.

Let me provide an example. If the dollar value of each box is three dollars and the price rises fifteen dollars then the chartist marks five boxes in a column matched to the prices shown on the vertical axis of the graph. Each time the price goes up another three dollars, another X is added to the same column, keeping pace with the prices noted on the left axis. If the price trend reverses, the chartist starts marking Os in the next column to the right (starting at the first declining price level) and continues to show price declines in that column (in three-dollar increments) until another reversal occurs.

As stated above, time does not play a role in the PF chart. Price movement is the only thing that matters. The Xs or Os continue to be added to the same column until the price reverses. In order to avoid small daily fluctuations, which would result in an unwieldy chart, the PF chartist may decide not to show a reversal unless the price has either risen or declined by a set amount.

I must apologize for the rather tortured paragraphs above. It is very difficult to describe a graph in words. If you go to the website Ehow. com, you can find a short video about the BC form of charting. A good presentation of the PF type of chart, with an example, can be seen at the website Stockcharts.com.

Assuming the technical analyst has been studying his or her chart of choice for a period and patterns are beginning to appear, then the analyst must decide what it all means. In his book *Stock Market Logic, A Sophisticated Approach to Profits on Wall Street*, Norman G. Fosback discusses chart patterns as follows:

> Because there is a potentially infinite number of price patterns that a stock can trace, chartists have identified (devised) a virtually infinite number of chart patterns to correspond to them. These patterns are known by such esoteric names as head and shoulders, reverse head and shoulders, single, double, and

triple tops and bottoms, flags, pennants, spikes, saucers, triangles, rectangles, lines, breakouts, consolidations, blowoffs; in short a name for everything and everything with a name.[5]

A chart covering a long period of price movement for an individual stock will begin to show trends up, down, or sideways. If the period shown on the chart is short term, the movements can be quite jagged. As the time lengthens, the chartist can trace a trend line along the price increases or declines shown on the chart. The trend line (starting from the left) over time is pointing northeast (going up), southeast (going down), or due east (staying the same) or reversing itself (inflection point). These are the basic messages a chart provides.

Over time relatively consistent highs and lows begin to show a stock's price range, which is defined by what is called the support level on the bottom, or the lowest point beyond which the price has not dropped in the applicable time period, and the resistance level on the top, or the highest point beyond which the price has not risen in the same period. This is the band within which the stock is trading. The chartist believes that a price break out above or below the price range is very predictive of the price trend in future trading. In effect the market may be in the process of setting new support or resistance levels. One of the basic principles of technical analysis is that a price break out either above the resistance level or below the support level or the occurrence of a sustained inflection point when the trend line reverses itself are all very important indicators. Depending on the volume accompanying such moves, the chart could be providing a strong indicator for the technical analyst to consider.

We must remember that the prices being charted show purchases and sales by people in the market. The support level reflects the price at which buyers have consistently come into the market to purchase shares of the stock. This would appear to be the price level at which the market considers the stock so cheap it is a buy. Conversely, resistance levels reflect the price above which no one is buying the stock—the price level at which the market considers the stock too expensive to buy. Any changes in these levels could be seen as changes in investor/trader sentiment about a stock. Technical analysts believe such changes foreshadow what people in the market may do in upcoming days, which could give the chartist a trading advantage.

If the price range band continues for a period, technical analysts refer to this as consolidation. During a period of consolidation, buyers and sellers seem to be indecisive as to which way the stock is going to move in the future, either up or down, since the trend line is flat. The stable price range might last for days, weeks, or months. During this period of neutrality, chartists look for indicators as to which way (up or down) the stock price might break out of the consolidation, which could signal the next trend.

If the price trend is going to resume its past direction, technical analysts believe the chart will show a pattern that looks like either a sloping flag or pennant. A flag forms a rectangle of prices, usually with a slope in the opposite direction from the previous rise or decline. A pennant is a triangular band, starting with wide price swings and converging at a point of small price changes, with no apparent directional slope. Each of these indicators tells the chartist the stock is taking a break before continuing to resume the previous price direction. The website StockCharts.com provides additional explanations and examples of flags and pennants. If the flags and pennants persist over a long period, the chartist may view the flag as a rectangle and the pennant as a symmetrical triangle—two other indicators.

If the trend is going to reverse itself and head in the opposite direction (a point of inflection), the chart might show a price pattern over time that looks like first a left shoulder then a higher head and finally a right shoulder: the head and shoulders pattern with alternating price rises and declines of varying heights and lengths.

A head and shoulders indicator, viewed in the normal pattern, is seen as a reversal from a trend of increasing prices to a trend of declining prices following the final movement of the right shoulder (downward). A reverse head and shoulders indicator, which looks the same but upside down, is viewed as the reversal from a trend of declining prices to a trend of increasing prices, following, again, the final movement of the right shoulder (upward).

MAKING A CHART

If a person has an interest in technical analysis, he or she would want to start studying charts. There are two ways to do that: seek advice or do it yourself. The person looking for advice could subscribe to a technical analyst's newsletter and follow the author's recommendations. The goal then becomes finding the newsletter that resonates with the individual with the hope of making at least enough money to pay the subscription fee. The do-it-yourself type must start by making a chart of the stock or the market in which he or she is interested. Whether it is a bar chart, a point and figure chart, a candlestick chart, or one of the many other types available, picking the form of chart is the first decision that must be made. The type of chart to use is a personal decision, much like the financial metrics selected by a fundamental analyst for his or her stock screen.

The computer has made charting a lot easier. The computer-literate chartist has several free stock chart websites from which to choose. Some of the top sites include StockCharts.com, Yahoo Finance, and Bigcharts.com. Google Finance also provides technical charting.

The old-fashioned way of charting involved pencil and graph paper with daily notations of the price movements of the chosen stock or market. Justin Mamis, in his book *The Nature of Risk, Stock Market Survival & The Meaning of Life*, had the following to say about making charts:

> You may not believe this, or want to accept it in this computerized era, but once you start keeping even a handful of charts yourself you'll see (and feel) the difference. The very nature

of how the stock is behaving rises to the surface via your pencil's posting the volume and the pattern. Of course, it's not perfect; it isn't even close to perfect. Sort of like Churchill's backhanded compliment about capitalism, **it's just better than anything else, and certainly better than nothing.** What happens is that the market "talks" to you as the language of its ticks becomes recordable on your chart paper. Keeping your own charts is the way the market's language can be heard most directly. To paraphrase a more important statement: All the rest of technical analysis is commentary.[6] [Author's emphasis in **bold.**]

Mr. Mamis repeated his advice about keeping your own chart in his later book, *When to Sell, Inside Strategies for Stock Market Profits.* Reminding his readers that charting did not take all that much time out of their day, he wrote: "It's taken you far longer to read this than it will to keep up with these statistics each day. We repeat: Don't rely on someone else to do what will take you so little time. You'll find you get a much better feel for what is actually happening by keeping your own hand and mind in."[7]

IT'S NOT PRICES; IT'S PEOPLE

We are almost finished with the technical aspects (the "how to") of technical analysis. The thing that must be remembered is that charts record market action, price, and volume, which is nothing more than the collective actions of the investors and traders in the market. Humphrey B. Neill explained it best in his 1931 classic *Tape Reading & Market Tactics.* Neill described the true purpose of technical analysis, or tape reading, as he called it, as follows:

In the first part of this book I have described the various kinds of people comprising the purchasers and sellers of stock. The important point to remember here is that all of those people are human beings, just as you and I are.

Let us get that picture clearly in mind. The ticker tape is simply **a record of human nature** passing in review. It is a record giving us the opinions and hopes of thousands of people. We must dismiss from our minds all other facts.[8] [Author's emphasis in **bold**.]

Technical analysis or charting in various forms has been around for scores of years. It went by a different name back in Neill's day. Back then technical analysts were referred to as tape readers. They received their market information from a ticker tape machine. The ticker tape machine, which was connected to stock exchanges over telegraph wires, printed out narrow strips of paper with stock trades, including stock symbols, prices, and volumes for all stock trades shortly after they were recorded on the floor of the stock exchange. All of the brokerage firms and stock trading shops had the machines in order to keep up with the daily market action almost as it happened.

The ticker tape machines provided stock trading reports on a delayed but close to real-time basis. Use of ticker tapes phased out when television and computers took over the job of providing virtually instantaneous market action. The streaming electronic boards with stock symbols, prices, and volumes on financial television broadcasts and in brokers' offices have replaced the old paper tape. The narrow strips of tape served a second purpose. They were used as confetti and thrown out office windows during parades on New York City streets. Hence the term *ticker tape parades*.

The heyday of the tape reader occurred in the early 1900s, when stock market manipulation (referred to then as operations) by secret investor pools and groups of corporate insiders was rampant. Back then the strategy was one of quiet accumulation and managed distribution of large amounts of a target stock. As the tape was received, the tape reader looked for price and volume movements that signaled that a stock market operation might be under way. The insightful trader would try to interpret what *they* were doing and buy the target stock to profit from the manipulated run up of a stock's price. The trader hoped to sell out his or her position before the inevitable crash of the stock after the group had unloaded all of their holdings on an unsuspecting public attracted to the stock by its market action. As I indicated above, it's really all about the people in the market.

In his famous economic text, *The General Theory of Employment, Interest and Money*, published in 1936, Professor Keynes described investing in a number of ways, all based on the idea that the successful investor is one who outwits the crowd. He likened investing to party games:

> For it is, so to speak, a game of Snap, of Old Maid, of Musical Chairs—a pastime in which he is victor who says Snap neither too soon nor too late, who passes the Old Maid to his neighbor before the game is over, who secures a chair for himself when the music stops.[9]

Keynes also compared investing to a popular newspaper contest of his time. The object of the competition was to pick out the prettiest faces from hundreds of photographs, with the prize going to the contestant who picked the faces also preferred by the entrants as a group. As Professor Keynes pointed out, the person picking the six prettiest had to decide which faces the group at large would choose when each of them is competing in the same way. He described the problem as follows: "It is not a case of choosing those which, to the best of one's judgment, are really the prettiest, nor even those which average opinion genuinely thinks the prettiest. We have reached the third degree where we devote our intelligence to anticipating what average opinion expects the average opinion to be. And there are some, I believe, who practice the fourth, fifth and higher degrees."[10]

This is the essence of technical analysis—learning from charts what the people in the market have been doing previously (maybe just an hour ago) with an eye to anticipating their next moves. The chartist's strategy is to take a trading position in a stock that appears most likely to either increase or decrease in price, netting a profit when the stock moves in the predicted direction.

TECHNICAL ANALYSIS/HANG GLIDING ACCORDING TO BURTON MALKIEL

In his book *A Random Walk Down Wall Street*, Professor Malkiel summed up technical analysis as follows:

> Technical analysis is essentially the making and interpreting of stock charts. Thus its practitioners, a small but abnormally devoted cult, are called chartists. They study the past—both the movements of common stock prices and the volume of trading—for a clue to the direction of future change...Most chartists believe that the market is only 10 percent logical and 90 percent psychological. They generally subscribe to the castle-in-the-air school and view the investment game as one of anticipating how the other players will behave. Charts, of course, tell only what the other players have been doing in the past. The chartist's hope, however, is that a careful study of what the other players are doing will shed light on what the crowd is likely to do in the future.[11]

It is interesting that Professor Malkiel refers to the stock market as "the investment game" and to the people trading and investing in it as "players." With a nod to Gustave Le Bon, he also refers to them as "the crowd."

Although he describes it accurately, Professor Malkiel does not have much respect for the technical form of investing. He referenced research into technical investment rules and reported the results:

> One set of tests, perhaps the simplest of all, compares the price change for a stock in a given period with the price change in a subsequent period. For example, technical lore has it that if the price of a stock rose yesterday, it is more likely to rise today. It turns out that the correlation of past price movements with present and future price movements is slightly positive but very close to zero. Last week's price change bears little relationship to the price change this week, and so forth. Whatever slight dependencies have been found between stock price movements in different time periods are extremely small and economically insignificant. Although there is some short-term momentum in the stock market, as will be described more fully in Chapter Ten, any investor who pays transaction costs cannot benefit from it. [12]

As I said, Professor Malkiel does not hold technical analysis in very high regard.

FUNDAMENTAL VERSUS TECHNICAL—OPPOSITES OR ALTERNATES

We have now completed our studies of fundamental and technical analyses. It may be presumptuous on my part, given my lack of exper-tise when compared to these eminent financial writers, but I would suggest fundamental and technical analyses may both have places in an investor's arsenal. An investor's personality will undoubtedly tend to bias his or her choice toward one or the other of the two strate-gies. A person with a deliberate bent for accounting data might not be attracted to the quick-draw nature of short-term, technical trading moves. Conversely, a person looking for rapid, "in and out" trading in the market will find a long-term fundamental approach utterly dull and smothering. So, to a certain extent, an individual's personality will probably lead him or her to either fundamental or technical ways of investing.

Notwithstanding the psychological attractions of each form of investing, all investors in the market share the common goal of making a profit. The follow-on to that common goal is the time it takes to book the profit. Viewed from this perspective, the issue of which form of investment strategy is the best might be recast as an exploration of an investor's goals and time horizons for the money available at the time. If a thirty-year-old, busy furthering his or her career, is investing for retirement and has little time or inclination to devote to the task, then a fundamental "buy it for keeps" approach may make the most sense. Finding a small portfolio of companies that meet all of his or her requirements for value investments may be all that is needed at this point in the person's investing career. That may change in the future, but for now such a strategy may fit the bill.

At some other point in time, and with funds to be devoted to a different investment goal, the same person, seeking a profit in a number of days, weeks, or months as opposed to retirement funds needed many years hence, may find a short-term technical strategy attractive. Please note the qualifier in that last sentence: "with funds to be devoted to a different investment goal" The money put into long-term, fundamental value investments for retirement is not disturbed. Different investment funds, which the person can afford to lose without suffering lasting financial damage, could be devoted to short-term technical trades.

To further complicate matters, fundamental and technical analyses are not the only options. In the next chapter, we will look at other investment strategies.

6

Additional Strategies and Conclusions

IS TIMING AS IMPORTANT ON WALL STREET AS IT IS IN LIFE?
It is basic human nature to seek order in chaos. Investors and speculators bring this instinct to their market moves. They try to make sense
out of the seemingly random action that occurs each day in the market.
One of the methods many market participants use to overcome this
market confusion is to ascribe a cyclical aspect to the market and then
time their trades in and out of the cycles as they unfold.

The mantra of market timing traders is "buy low, sell high."
Essentially, market timing is asset allocation—that is, switching your
investment funds in and out of equities and interest-bearing securities
(corporate or government debt instruments) to avoid market declines
and capture market tops. When the market has peaked, you sell your
stocks and buy bonds. When the market has bottomed out, you reverse
course, sell the bonds, and reinvest in stocks. One market researcher
studied the stock market from 1946 through 1991. He calculated that
the annual overall market return for this forty-five-year period was
11.2 percent. His research showed that if an investor had been able to
move his funds in a timely manner out of the stock market and avoid
the period's fifty worst months and then get back in (again on a timely
basis), the annual return on his funds would have been 19 percent, an
increase that would certainly have warranted the effort.

If it were only that easy. How does a trader decide that the bad times are coming? More importantly, how does he or she decide it's time to jump back into stocks?

Technical analysts look at volumes and prices of stocks they follow. Market timers look at the same statistics but on a marketwide basis. If the volume of the overall market is heavy and price advances rapid across the board, the timer looks to pick the top at which he or she sells all equity positions ahead of the anticipated decline. Conversely, when volumes are thin and prices appear totally depressed, the timer sells his or her bonds and moves back into the market, buying equities in anticipation of the upward swing of prices. The market timer might trade index funds representing the S&P 500 or the Russell 2000 Indexes. There are as many indexes as there are market groups. There are bond funds of various types to use when it appears to be time to leave equities. I am sure timers have other strategies as well. Indeed, there are market-timing mutual funds run by money managers who specialize in this form of trading.

Both investors and traders keep their eyes on the relationship between prevailing interest rates for debt instruments and the anticipated returns of equities. If bonds offer returns higher than those of equities by a substantial amount, an individual may conclude that now is the time to load up on debt securities. Professor Burton G. Malkiel described this tension between debt and equities as follows:

> The stock market, no matter how much it may think so, does not exist as a world unto itself. Investors should consider how much profit they can obtain elsewhere. Interest rates, if they are high enough, offer a stable, profitable alternative to the stock market. Consider periods such as the early 1980s when yields on prime quality corporate bonds soared to close to 15 percent. Long-term bonds of

somewhat lower quality were being offered at even higher interest rates. The expected returns from stock prices had trouble matching these bond rates; money flowed into bonds while stock prices fell sharply. Finally, stock prices reached such a low level that a sufficient number of investors were attracted to stem the decline. Again, in 1987, interest rates rose substantially, preceding the great stock market crash of October 19. To put it another way, to attract investors from high-yielding bonds, stocks must offer bargain-basement prices.

A rational investor should be willing to pay a higher price for a share, other things being equal, the lower are interest rates.[1]

The market timer has two negatives to overcome with this strategy. Brokerage commissions and fees can put a drag on returns if there is a good deal of trading, and this activity, in turn, generates income taxes. Both of these trading costs need to be accounted for when calculating the true return on the investments. There are also some nontechnical (and amusing) timing strategies.

The American author Mark Twain is best known for his many books and essays on life as he saw it. He also had some ideas about the stock market: "October. This is one of the peculiarly dangerous months to speculate in stocks in. The others are July, January, September, April, November, May, March, June, December, August and February."[2]

If you look long and hard enough, you will find some degree of correlation between all sorts of apparently unrelated events. Based on a study for the years between 1949 and 1975, some analysts feel there is a connection between the behavior of the market in January and the rest of that year. The old saying is "as January goes, so goes the year." Interestingly, prior to 1949, January's action was accurately predictive only 50 percent of the time, equivalent to a coin toss. I suspect the study's period stopped in 1975 for the same reason.

Some believe that politics may have an effect on the markets. In a recent article in *The Wall Street Journal*, it was reported that the Dow Jones Industrial Average has recorded a 7.8 percent yearly gain under Democratic presidents and only a 3 percent gain per year under Republicans since 1900. A 9.6 percent average annual gain was reported during the terms of every Democratic president faced with a Republican Congress.

Two of the more lighthearted market timing predictors are the Super Bowl effect and the Hemline Index. The Super Bowl effect is the proposition that if an NFL team wins the Super Bowl, the market will do well that year. If an AFL team wins, the market is in for a decline. The Hemline Index is based on the length of women's dresses and skirts, which are seen as indicators of the market. If the skirts are rising, so too will the market. Conversely, if skirt lengths are heading to the ankles, a market decline is in the offing. Not to put too fine a point on this one, but there is a limit as to how high a woman's skirt can rise. The same certainly holds true for the market. Like dresses, markets cannot rise forever. At best you might be able to say hemlines rise during good times when people are happy, optimistic, and eager to invest. They drop when the mood of the people becomes somber (because markets are declining?). I would strongly advise against betting your life savings on either of these indices.

Norman G. Fosback, in his book *Stock Market Logic, A Sophisticated Approach to Profits on Wall Street*, wrote about timing and cycles. His conclusion was noted earlier, but bears repeating: "In the meantime, if cycles have a utility, it is in reminding us that 'This, too, shall pass;' that no bull market or bear market lasts forever."[3]

I will end with another quote from Mark Twain: "There are two times in a man's life when he should not speculate: when he can't afford it, and when he can."[4]

LOOKING FOR ACTION—MOMENTUM TRADING

Momentum trading is based on two concepts.

The first is that investors are slow to react to news about a company or its stock. Unexpected stock price movements, earnings announcements, or other surprising company news (whether good or bad) may trigger a move in the company's stock that will continue for a period of time after the announcement as investors analyze the news and decide how to react. As stated earlier, Humphrey B. Neill, in his book *The Art of Contrary Thinking*, pointed out that it is basic human nature to cling to a belief in a market trend for a period after that movement has come to an end. The momentum trader looks to quickly jump into the stock early in the move and sell out of the stock with a profit shortly thereafter. Momentum trading based on announcements has a time horizon measured in hours or, at most, a day or two. Because the stock movement is usually small, in relative terms, many momentum traders use margin to increase the amount of profit they hope to gain. Some traders try to jump the gun by following the old Wall Street adage "buy on the rumor; sell on the news."

The second rule for momentum trading is "the trend is your friend." The trader looks for stocks with a large degree of relative strength. The trader may compare the stock's current velocity of price change to its average rate of change over the past few months. If the stock has been moving in a direction at a price change rate of one dollar per week and is now trading at an increased rate of five dollars per week, it could look like a candidate for a momentum trade. It is also possible to compare a stock's rate of price change to the average rate for other stocks in its industry or in the overall market. Similarly, the momentum trader may look for stocks with unusually high trading volume. A stock that normally trades ten thousand shares a day and is now trading one hundred thousand shares a day will attract the attention of the momentum trader. These traders may also look for a chart indicator showing a point of inflection—that is, the point at which the stock's trading trend will reverse. As we learned earlier, this point of inflection is best demonstrated by the head and shoulders technical indicator.

Successful momentum traders have two characteristics. First, they have the time to devote to the constant monitoring of their stock positions throughout the day. Second, they will trade out of a stock at a loss very quickly if the movement is going against them. The big profit on one trade is supposed to make up for the small losses of other trades. Momentum trading, therefore, is a strategy for professionals who are in the market on a daily basis and are willing to suffer any number of small losses as a cost of doing business. It is not a strategy for the part-time amateur. I suspect there may be mutual funds using momentum trading as their primary strategy.

Ben Graham and his student, Warren Buffett, are considered icons of fundamental analysis and value investing. Market timers, chartists, and momentum traders also have their hero: Jesse Lauriston Livermore, who was known early in his career as the "Boy Plunger" and later as the "Great Bear of Wall Street."

Livermore was born in Massachusetts in 1877. He started his career at the age of fourteen posting stock quotes for a Boston brokerage firm. He made his first money trading in bucket shops. A bucket shop was a form of stock market casino in which the patrons could make bets on stocks with little money down and large margins (borrowed money). The shop did not really buy or sell the stocks picked by the customers but rather paid off winning stock picks (much like a horse track).

Livermore made and lost millions during his career. Having succeeded by short selling during the stock market panic of 1907, he recognized the signs of pending decline in 1929. He again shorted the market successfully during the October 1929 crash. It is said he had a net worth of $100 million (in 1929 dollars) after the most famous market crash in American history.

The author and journalist Edwin Lefevre is credited with writing the ever-popular book *Reminiscences of a Stock Operator*, first published in 1923. It is believed he collaborated with Jesse Livermore on writing the book, which is a thinly veiled biography of the famous trader, recounting many of his triumphs and losses. Most importantly the author provides detailed descriptions and explanations of his trading strategies in a first-person, conversational writing style. Livermore later claimed to have written the book with Lefevre serving as editor. In any event Livermore also wrote a book under his own name, *How to Trade Stocks*, which was published shortly before his death in 1940. Both books remain in print today.

The main character in Lefevre's book, Larry Livingston, recounted several general rules about the market and traders. In discussing the market, he wrote:

> Nowhere does history indulge in repetitions so often or so uniformly as in Wall Street. When you read contemporary accounts of booms and panics, the one thing that strikes you most forcibly is how little either stock speculation or stock speculators today differ from yesterday. The game does not change and neither does human nature.
>
> Weapons change, but strategy remains strategy, on the New York Stock Exchange as on the battlefield. I think the clearest summing up of the whole thing was expressed by Thomas F. Woodlock when he declared: "The principles of successful stock speculation are based on the supposition that people will continue in the future to make the mistakes that they have made in the past."[5]

The four most dangerous words on Wall Street? "This time, it's different."

Most market watchers think the two underlying causes of market action are fear and greed. Livingston looked at it differently:

> The speculator's chief enemies are always boring from within. It is inseparable from human nature to hope and to fear. In speculation when the market goes against you, you hope that every day will be the last day—and you lose more than you should had you not listened to hope—to the same ally that is so potent a success-bringer to empire builders and pioneers, big and little. And when the market goes your way, you become fearful that the next day will take away your profit, and you get out—too soon. Fear keeps you from making as much money as you ought to. The successful trader has to fight these two deep-seated instincts. He has to reverse what you might call his natural impulses. Instead of hoping he must fear; instead of fearing he must hope. He must fear that his loss will develop into a much bigger loss and hope that his profit may become a big profit. It is absolutely wrong to gamble in stocks the way the average man does.[6]

The main character and narrator in Lefevre's book believed that tape reading was not as complicated as it seemed. He used the tape to determine if the tendency of prices, the trend, indicated it was time to buy (go long) or sell (go short). He described it as follows: "Prices, we know, will move either up or down according to the resistance they encounter. For purposes of easy explanation we will say that prices, like everything else, move along the line of least resistance. They will do whatever comes easiest, therefore they will go up if there is less resistance to an advance than to a decline; and vice versa."[7]

In addition he advised traders to be patient and wait until the market direction was very clear and then to join in the movement, being careful not to get caught at the top of a market ready to crash. He put it best when he wrote, "One of the most helpful things that anybody can learn is to give up trying to catch the last eighth—or the first. These two are the most expensive eighths in the world."[8] He referenced eighths (12.5 cents) because in 1923 stock prices were posted in fractions, not in today's decimals.

EARLY DAYS MARKET OPERATIONS

In Lefevre's classic, Larry Livingston recounted several market manipulations he was involved in over the years. I should point out that at that time, there were few rules in effect concerning various market strategies that today would violate securities laws and the rules of the Securities and Exchange Commission. Here is what Mr. Livingston had to say about his trading strategies:

> The word "manipulation" has come to have an ugly sound. It needs an alias. I do not think there is anything so very mysterious or crooked about the process itself when it has for an object the selling of a stock in bulk, provided, of course, that such operations are not accompanied by misrepresentation. Usually the object of manipulation is to develop marketability—that is, the ability to dispose of fair-sized blocks at some price at any time.
>
> In the majority of cases the object of manipulation is, as I said, to sell stock to the public at the best possible price. It is not alone a question of selling, but of distributing. There is no sense in marking up the price to a very high level if you cannot induce the public to take it off your hands later. Let me start at the beginning. Assume that there is some one—an underwriting syndicate or a pool or an individual—that has a block of stock which it is desired to sell at the best price possible. The best place for selling it ought to be the open market, and the

best buyer ought to be the general public. Suppose he has heard of me as a man who knows the game. He then arranges for an interview, and in due time calls at my office. My visitor tells me what he and his associates wish to do, and asks me to undertake the deal.

I generally ask and receive calls (call options) on a block of stock. I insist upon graduated calls as the fairest to all concerned. The price of the call begins at a little below the prevailing market price and goes up; say, for example, that I get calls on one hundred thousand shares and the stock is quoted at 40. I begin with a call for some thousands of shares at 35, another at 37, another at 40, and at 45 and 50, and so on up to 75 or 80. If as the result of my professional work—my manipulation—the price goes up, and if at the highest level there is a good demand for the stock so that I can sell fair-sized blocks of it I of course call the stock. I am making money; but so are my clients making money. This is as it should be.

The first step in a bull movement in a stock is to advertise the fact that there is a bull movement on. Sounds silly, doesn't it? Well, think a moment. It isn't as silly as it sounded, is it? The most effective way to advertise what, in effect, are your honorable intentions is to make the stock active and strong. After all is said and done, the greatest publicity agent in the wide world is the ticker, and by far the best advertising medium is the tape. I accomplish all these highly desirable things by merely making the stock active. When there is activity there is a synchronous demand for explanations; and that means, of course, that the necessary reasons—for publication—supply themselves without the slightest aid from me.

Activity is all that the floor traders ask. They will buy or sell any stock at any level if only there is a free market for it. They will deal in thousands of shares wherever they see activity, and their aggregate capacity is considerable. It necessarily happens that they constitute the manipulator's first crop of buyers.

To get a professional following, I myself have never had to do more than to make a stock active. Traders don't ask for more. It is well, of course, to remember that these professionals on the floor of the Exchange buy stocks with the intention of selling them at a profit. They do not insist on its being a big profit; but it must be a quick profit.

I make the stock active in order to draw the attention of speculators to it, for the reasons I have given. I buy it and I sell it and the traders follow suit. The selling pressure is not apt to be strong where a man has as much speculatively held stock sewed up—in calls—as I insist on having. The buying, therefore, prevails over the selling, and the public follows the lead not so much of the manipulator as of the room traders.

As the market broadens I of course sell stock on the way up, but never enough to check the rise. It is obvious that the more stock I sell on a reasonable and orderly advance the more I encourage the conservative speculators, who are more numerous than the reckless room traders; and in addition, the more support I shall be able to give the stock on the inevitable weak days.

I repeat that at no time during the manipulation do I forget to be a stock trader. My problems as a manipulator, after all, are the same that confront me as an operator. All manipulation comes to an end when the manipulator cannot make a stock do what he wants it to do. Don't argue with the tape. Do not seek to lure the profit back. Quit while the quitting is good—and cheap.[9]

Although Livermore claimed authorship of *Reminiscences*, I believe that Edwin Lefevre actually wrote the book in collaboration with him. To me there is a vast difference in writing styles between *Reminiscences* and the book *How to Trade in Stocks*, written by Jesse Livermore in 1940.

LIVING ON THE MARGIN

A loan from a stockbroker to finance a stock purchase is called margin. These loans are also referred to as call loans since they can be terminated, or called, at any time by the lending broker. Short sellers borrow stock instead of money, but it is still the same thing, a loan known as margin. The amount an individual can borrow is limited by the amount of equity—that is, the combined value of all of the securities in the person's stock account less any existing margin debt. In the United States, the percentage of margin available to the account owner is set by the Federal Reserve Bank (FRB). Stock exchanges and individual brokerage firms have their own rules as well, but they take the lead from the FRB. The margin percentage has changed over the years depending on whether the FRB wants to depress or stimulate stock market action. The lower the margin rate, the more people can borrow; the higher the rate, the less they can borrow. The initial margin requirement rate today is 50 percent for common stocks. As with any other loan, the broker charges interest on the margined amount.

In addition to margin limits, only certain securities are marginable, which means they qualify as collateral for the margin loan. The broker can sell these securities to cover the margin loan if their values decline to the point that the available collateral value is less than the required amount. If the stocks decline in price, the broker contacts the customer and demands additional collateral (cash) be deposited in the account— a margin call. If the customer does not respond on a timely basis, the broker sells enough securities in the account to pay down the loan. It is said that one of the primary causes of the 1929 Wall Street crash was a continuous loop of unmet margin calls that triggered immediate stock sales by brokers resulting in further reduced stock prices, which led to another round of unmet margin calls, stock sales, and price declines, over and over in a vicious circle.

What is the attraction of margin? Assume you have $10,000 to invest in a stock trading at fifty dollars per share. Ignoring fees, commissions, and interest charges, you can buy two hundred shares. If the stock is marginable at a 50 percent rate, you can buy four hundred shares with your $10,000 plus the additional margin of $10,000 lent to you by your broker. One year later the stock is trading at seventy-five dollars per share, and you sell at a profit. If you had not used margin and had purchased only two hundred shares with your $10,000, you would have a profit of $5,000 ($15,000–$10,000 basis). With the sale of your four hundred margin shares, your profit is $10,000 ($30,000–$20,000 basis and margin). A $5,000 profit on a $10,000 investment is a 50 percent return on your investment. A $10,000 profit on your $10,000 investment is a 100 percent return, again ignoring fees and interest charges.

If your stock had dropped to twenty-five dollars per share, the losses are magnified as well. If you had purchased the two hundred shares, you would still own stock worth $5,000 in your account. If you had purchased an additional two hundred shares on margin and the broker issued a margin call that you did not meet, the broker would have sold all the stock to cover the price decline (four hundred shares at twenty-five dollars equals $10,000). You would have nothing left. In reality you would have lost more than your $10,000 since the broker would demand payment of all the fees, commissions, and interest charges we ignored in our example.

Professor John Kenneth Galbraith wrote *The Great Crash 1929* in 1955 and explained the purpose of margin from the broker's perspective as follows:

The purpose is to accommodate the speculator and facilitate speculation. But the purposes cannot be admitted. Margin trading must be defended not on the grounds that it efficiently and ingeniously assists the speculator, but that it encourages the extra trading which changes a thin and anemic market into a thick and healthy one. At best this is a dull by-product and a dubious one. Wall Street, in these matters, is like a lovely and accomplished woman who must wear black cotton stockings, heavy woolen underwear, and parade her knowledge as a cook because, unhappily, her supreme accomplishment is as a harlot.[10]

Humphrey B. Neill, in his book *Tape Reading & Market Tactics*, advised his readers as follows: "The Market Philosopher's advice to his class is: **never answer a margin-call**. Tell your broker to sell enough of the shares he is holding for you to meet his requirements. The margin-clerk is your best friend: he can be depended upon to tell you when to sell; and if you do not follow his tip, he will sell anyway"[11] (Author's emphasis in **bold**).

As with every other investment strategy we have looked at, it all comes down to what makes the most sense to you as an individual investor. If you decide to invest on margin, remember Neill's advice, and never return that call from your broker.

SHORT SELLING

As pointed out earlier by Justin Mamis, most investors and traders are optimistic (or at least hopeful) that the prices of the stocks they purchase will rise. They make their money when the price increases (bulls). A minority of individuals, however, are equally convinced that prices of some stocks are destined to decline (bears). They invest with the goal of making money on price declines. They are the short sellers.

A short sale is a speculation for traders, not long-term investors. The trader believes that the price of a particular stock is going to decline. The trader borrows stock shares from a broker and sells them in the market. The buyer of the stock does not know or care if the shares he or she has purchased were borrowed. For example, assume you believe a stock is about to decline. You borrow one thousand shares of the stock from a broker and sell them at fifty dollars per share. You now have a credit balance in your account of $50,000 (we'll ignore the fees, interest charges, and commissions). If, as you believe, the price of the stock drops to thirty dollars per share, you buy one thousand shares in the market for $30,000 and return them to the broker. Your account still has $20,000 in it, all profit. If the stock goes up to sixty dollars and you decide to close out the transaction, you have to buy the shares you owe the broker at a cost of $60,000. You have to add $10,000 to the $50,000 in your account to complete the purchase. The additional $10,000 deposit plus the fees, commissions, and interest represent your loss.

The famous trader Jesse Lauriston Livermore explained in his 1940 book *How to Trade in Stocks* why he engaged in short selling: "There is no good direction to trade, short or long, there is only the 'money making' way to trade. But the stock market moves up roughly a third of the time, sideways a third of the time, and downward a third of the time. If you only played the bull-side of the market, you were out of the action, and a chance to make money two thirds of the time."[12]

Livermore emphasized the fact that a trader, whether selling (going short) or buying (going long), had to pay constant attention to the trend of a stock, not its price. Just because a price has moved seemingly a great deal does not mean it can't continue to drop or rise even more.

Short sellers are not very popular on Wall Street. Fred Schwed, Jr. described this in his 1940 book *Where Are the Customers' Yachts?* with the following:

I recall reading a novel about a rich man who was in everything vicious and hateful. Among his evil attributes the author described how he had made his first fortune. He had "sold stocks short during a great panic and had thus enriched himself fabulously while hundreds of thousands were being plunged into poverty and ruin."

This quotation expresses well enough the vague, universal indignation at the short seller. (This indignation only exists during and after panics—during prosperous times he receives about as much attention as do people who practice barratry. Before October, 1929, no one objected to short sellers except their own families. The families objected to going bankrupt.)

Vague as the general feeling is, two of its implications are quite clear. One is that being a bear raider is something like being a usurer or a jewel thief—that it is an easy way to pick up a fortune provided you are willing to be immoral. The second is that it is socially harmful.

Before examining these two claims, I must touch on the ancient human tendency to personify general misfortune in some human shape. While "hundreds of thousands are being plunged into poverty" only the thoughtful ask, "What is happening to us?" The popular cry is "**Who** is doing this to us?" and its satisfying sequel—"Just let me get my hands on him!"[13] [Author's emphasis in **bold**.]

I think that short selling is best left to market professionals speculating throughout the day in the market. It is not a game for amateurs trading on a part-time basis.

OPTIONS, FUTURES, AND FANTASY FOOTBALL
Professional football is one of the most popular sports in America. Not satisfied with just betting on their favorite teams, sports fanatics developed fantasy football. In its most basic form, participants create

fantasy teams with real players from the NFL. The performance of a person's fantasy team, measured in points, is derived from the weekly performance over the season of the players he or she has picked. The owner of the fantasy team with the most points at the end of the real season wins the prize pool. National companies have recently started offering the public the opportunity to play fantasy football on a weekly basis with the possibilty of winning millions if they choose the NFL players with the best performances at their positions in that week's games.

There is a similar investment game played every day on various exchanges devoted to options and futures. On an options/futures exchange, people buy or sell financial instruments, the values of which are based upon—or, to be more accurate, derived from—the values of their underlying securities. Such financial instruments are generally referred to as derivatives. One derivative, an option, comes in two forms: the right to buy an asset at a fixed price (a call option) and the right to sell the asset at a fixed price (a put option). In either case the option expires at a predetermined time, after which it is no longer enforceable.

Although derivatives like options may seem to be modern financial tools, such is not the case. Aristotle told a story about one of the first Greek philosophers, Thales of Miletus (circa 624 BC–546 BC). Unlike most of his contemporaries, Thales believed weather was a natural phenomenon; not a message sent by the gods to show pleasure or anger. As the story goes, one year most folks believed the gods were angry and that the god-sent weather would result in a bad olive crop. Believing otherwise, Thales went to olive-press owners in the area in the spring and purchased the exclusive right (option) to use their presses in the fall. Since the owners believed their presses would be sitting idle at harvest, they gladly took his money. As Thales suspected, the weather was fine, and the olive growers had a bumper crop. Thales had the right to charge the olive growers whatever he wanted for the use of the presses and, reportedly, did so.

A call option for a stock gives the purchaser of the option the right to purchase one hundred shares of a stock for a fixed price (the strike or exercise price) for a set period (the life of the option). The purchaser pays the going market price for the option. The purchaser of the call is betting that the price of the underlying asset, such as a stock, will increase beyond the strike price. The purchaser can then exercise the option and sell the stock at the higher price in the market. The allure of the call option for the purchaser is that the amount of profit is hypo-thetically unlimited, but the amount of the loss is limited to the option price paid at the beginning of the contract.

As we know, for every buyer there must be a seller. The seller of a call option receives the option price paid by the purchaser. The seller is betting that the price of the stock does not go above the strike price by the expiration of the life of the option. If the market price of the stock does not beat the strike price by the end of the option's life, the seller of the call option keeps the money the purchaser paid for the option. Aside from accepting the risk, the option price the seller receives can be seen as free money. If the market price of the stock at the end of the time for exercise remains below the strike price, the purchaser has lost only the money paid to the seller for the option. If the market price of the stock at the end of the exercise period is above the strike price, the purchaser calls for the stock at the strike price from the seller of the option and resells it at the market price for a profit.

Assuming the seller of the option had to go into the market to buy the stock to fulfill the option contract, the seller of the option now has a loss—that is, the difference between the current stock price he or she has to pay for the stock less the option price received and the strike price—that is, the amount paid by the purchaser upon exercise of the option. There is one instance in which the call option results in a win-win for both parties. Assume the seller of the call option already owns the stock, and the strike price would result in a gain he or she is willing to accept in any event. If the option expires, the seller has the option price. If the option is exercised, the seller has the anticipated gain on the sale of the stock plus the option price.

A put option is the exact opposite of a call option. A put option gives the purchaser of the option the right to sell one hundred shares of a stock to the seller of the option for the strike price for the life of the option. The purchaser of a put pays the market price for the option. The purchaser of a put option is betting that the price of the stock will decline below the strike price. The purchaser can then exercise the option, buy the stock in the market at the lower price, and put it to the seller of the put option at the strike price for a profit. Just like the seller of a call option, the seller of a put option hopes the option will expire without being exercised, allowing him or her to pocket the price paid for the option. If the seller of a put option bets wrong, he or she is obligated to buy the stock at the strike price, which would be above market price at the time of exercise.

So, to make things simple, if you think a stock price is going to rise, you can buy the stock itself, you can buy a call option on the stock at a strike price you think the stock price will ultimately exceed, or you could sell a put option, which, if the price rises, will expire unexercised, and you pocket the option price. If you think a stock price is going to decline, you can short the stock itself, you can buy a put option on the stock at a strike price you think the stock price will decline below, or you can sell a call option, which, if the price does not reach the strike price, will expire unexercised, and, again, you pocket the option price.

The option trader is risking a lot less money than if he or she went into the market to buy a stock, or to short it. In the case of the purchaser of either a call option or a put option, the loss is limited to the price paid for the option. The risk of loss is hypothetically unlimited for the seller of either type of option; however, the option price represents found money received by a seller who is convinced the stock price will act as the seller anticipates and the option will expire unexercised,

Another popular derivative is the forward contract. With an option the purchaser has the right to fulfill the call or put contract. With a forward contract, the purchaser has the obligation to fulfill an agreement for the purchase or sale of a commodity or a financial asset at a set price now. The purchaser need not pay for the asset until a later date, the settlement or expiration date. This would be the basic form of agreement between a farmer and a grain processor. The farmer has locked in the price to be paid and the profit to be made at harvest. The processor has fixed his cost for the grain in advance.

A futures contract is much like a forward contract but with one important difference. With a futures contract, any gains or losses that might accrue as the current market price varies from the futures price are realized daily, not at the settlement date. This daily accounting is referred to as the mark to market accounting principle. Another difference is that both parties to a futures contract have to post a bond or make a deposit, with the broker acting as the intermediary in the contract to ensure their performance at the end of the contract. This deposit or bond is called the initial margin, and it generally ranges between 2 percent and 10 percent of the contract value, depending on the volatility of the asset. Since each party has to mark to market at the end of every day, the broker may call upon a person with a losing position to deposit more money in his or her account.

Futures contracts have standard provisions relating to the settlement date and the size of the contract, which allows them to be freely traded on exchanges. The majority of traded contracts are futures contracts. Forward contracts tend to be customized to the needs of the parties. Consequently they are not normally traded on exchanges.

Rather, they are established through forward-contract brokers who act as intermediaries.

DOES MY MONEY NEED A PASSPORT?

Once upon a time, corporate America was top dog and paid little attention to the industries of other countries and their products. Then change started to happen. People began driving Volkswagens and Toyotas instead of Chevys and Oldsmobiles. Some bikers bought Honda motorcycles instead of Harleys. Sony televisions became market leaders, pushing aside Zenith and Magnavox. Pasta actually came from Italy. You could find excellent wines from South America at your local liquor store at reasonable prices. Chocolate lovers traded their Baby Ruth bars for Nestle Crunch. Interestingly, Baby Ruth bars are now made by Nestle. Globalization hit with a vengeance and continues to this day.

One of the earliest pioneers in international investing was Sir John Templeton. Born in Tennessee, Templeton ultimately moved to Nassau, where he became a naturalized British citizen. He was knighted for his work in several fields, including philanthropy. He formed the Templeton World Fund in 1978, one of the first mutual funds to invest on a global basis. Templeton had a value/contrarian investment strategy. Unlike most of his contemporaries, however, he would look for low-priced companies beyond America's shores. He is considered one of the top international investors in the history of Wall Street.

Peter Lynch managed the Fidelity Magellan Fund for thirteen years with an astounding average return of 29 percent per annum. A little-known fact is that a portion of that return was attributable to his foreign investments. In his book *Beating the Street*, he revealed what he called his "adventures abroad" as follows:

> With the exception of John Templeton, I was the first domestic fund manager to invest heavily in foreign stocks. Templeton's

fund was a global version of Magellan. Whereas I might
have 10-20 percent of the money invested in foreign stocks,
Templeton invested most of his money abroad.

With the pile of cash I now had to invest, I was almost
forced to turn to foreign stocks, particularly in Europe. With a
big fund, I needed to find big companies that would make big
moves, and Europe has a higher percentage of big companies
than we do.[13]

So, what does this mean for the individual investor? Many Wall Street
professionals advise their clients to diversify a portion of their portfolios with the stocks of foreign companies.

It has been reported that 54 percent of investment-grade stocks in
the world, based on capitalization, are located in countries other than
the United States. Of the ten largest car manufacturers in the world,
only two of them are American (Chrysler is owned by Fiat). Similarly,
seven of the ten largest companies engaged in telecommunications are
in other countries. Half of the ten largest household-products manufacturers are located outside the United States, but their products
are available here. The vast majority of mining operations are found
overseas.

If an individual investor has decided that a portion of his or her
portfolio should be invested in foreign stocks, there are several alterna-
tives available. International investing can be accomplished with mutual
funds, exchange-traded funds (ETFs), American depository receipts
(ADRs), and direct investing in a foreign market. The costs, expenses,
and difficulties of directly trading a stock in a foreign market put this
strategy out of the reach of most individuals.

Mutual funds and ETFs investing overseas come in two varieties.
A global fund invests in companies throughout the world. This means a
portion of the fund will hold stocks in the investor's own country. If the

fund is labeled *international* or *foreign*, there will be no stocks from the investor's country in the portfolio.

Some mutual funds and ETFs invest only in developed countries, such as the United States, England, France, Japan, and Germany. Others focus on emerging markets, or less developed countries with prospects for increased rates of growth. In 2003 the investment firm Goldman Sachs identified Brazil, Russia, India, and China as the four emerging markets with the greatest potential to become dominant in the global economy. The countries are collectively referred to by the acronym BRIC. Goldman projected that China and India would together lead the world in manufacturing, and Russia and Brazil would become leading suppliers of raw materials. These countries are, obviously, not a political bloc. However, if they worked together financially, they could become a very powerful economic force in the global economy by 2050. Some predict that BRIC could surpass today's economic powers, including the United States.

The investment firm JP Morgan introduced ADRs to American investors in 1927. This was one of the first ways to invest internationally in this country. An investment firm purchases and holds large amounts of foreign stocks in safekeeping. It then sells shares, or receipts, in that portfolio (much like a mutual fund) to US investors. Those receipts are traded on Wall Street in US dollars, just like US stocks. These days some of the larger foreign companies cut out the middleman, the investment firm sponsoring the ADRs, and issue their shares directly into the US markets.

International investing brings added risks. Since foreign companies are not necessarily subject to the disclosure requirements imposed on US companies by the Securities and Exchange Commission, financial information can be difficult to get and may not be entirely reliable. Political instability in emerging countries could detrimentally affect companies in those countries. There are many examples of companies being nationalized by foreign governments. Currency exchange rates fluctuate daily, which can impact the US dollar value of a foreign investment. Inflation rates vary from country to country and could drive down the value of a foreign stock held by an American investor even though the actual business of the company has not changed.

There is one last thing for you to keep in mind. US companies are increasingly becoming global in their own right. Approximately half of the companies in the S&P 500 Index break out global sales in their financial reports. Global revenues of the reporting companies represented 46 percent of their total revenues in 2012. Therefore almost 25 percent of all S&P 500 revenues for this group of companies could be seen to come from foreign countries in that year. If you assume that the same percentages held true for the companies that did not break out their foreign business, it could be that almost 50 percent of the revenue of the S&P 500 companies was international in 2012. Obviously the percentage changes annually, but if this is truly the case, an individual investor might safely invest internationally by simply buying an S&P 500 Index mutual fund or ETF.

THE DARK SIDE OF MARKETS

Any time you mix people, money, and uncertain outcomes (sounds like Wall Street, doesn't it?), there will always be a certain number of participants looking for the easy (illegal) way to make money.

Fred Schwed, Jr. discussed the issue of fraud on Wall Street in his book *Where Are the Customers' Yachts? or A Good Hard Look At Wall Street*. He felt that the public's widely held feeling that their losses were the result of dishonesty were overblown and, to a certain extent, self-serving. He wrote about public opinion of Wall Street inhabitants:

> The public feels that Wall Streeters are not dunces at all; that they are crooks and scoundrels and very clever ones at that;

that they sell for millions what they know is worthless; in short, that they are villains, not children.

The burnt customer certainly prefers to believe that he has been robbed rather than that he has been a fool on the advice of fools. Even Wall Street men themselves tend to encourage the idea.

The crookedness of Wall Street is in my opinion an over-rated phenomenon. The hearts of Wall Street men are not more or less black than the hearts of the men in the sausage-cover game. There is probably the same percentage of malpractice, but the Wall Street depredations are more spectacular. They involve vastly greater sums, and they make more interesting reading. Best of all, they suggest to the public an excuse for the public's own folly. [14]

Fraud is, indeed, occasionally practiced on Wall Street; however, I believe that much larger losses are incurred much more frequently by thoughtless, emotional investing by the public. Schwed made the following comments concerning the Securities and Exchange Commission, established after the 1929 market crash and subsequent depression in the United States:

Wall Street needed the S.E.C. just like baseball after 1919 needed Commissioner Landis. But people who are interested in baseball are more realistic than people interested in Wall Street. The fans did not expect Judge Landis would do more for the game than keep it reasonably honest. They did not expect him to improve the quality of the fielding and hitting. Nevertheless, a considerable part of the public seems to be expecting the S.E.C. will make speculation and investment safer.

These hopeful individuals are reminiscent of the benevolent soul who said at the beginning of the poker game, "Now, boys, if we all play carefully we can all win a little."[15]

BLIND MEN AND THE ELEPHANT

We have now learned about various forms of investment analysis. The proponents of each form of investing not only tout the merits of their preferred method but spend almost as much time and effort denigrating the others. I am reminded of the old parable about a group of blind men and an elephant. This is a common story found in Buddhist, Sufi Muslim, Hindu, and other religious/philosophical writings.

Supposedly originating in India centuries ago, the basic story focuses on blind men who are told to describe the king's elephant. The catch, of course, is that each individual can explore only one part of the animal, and none of the men can touch the same part. In each version of the parable, the men report their findings to the king. The man who felt the leg describes the animal as a pillar. The man who grabbed the tail imagines the elephant as a rope. The one who explored the trunk reports that the elephant is like a large tree branch. Conflicting reports are also provided by the individuals who touched the stomach, an ear, and a tusk. The men argue about who is correct. The king resolves the dispute by explaining that each of them is correct based on what they touched (their individual perspectives); however, none of them is totally correct.

Like the elephant and its many parts, the market has many different investments to offer to investors and speculators. Investors and speculators differ in many ways but are the same in certain respects. Each one has a goal, a preferred method of achieving that goal, and a time frame within which to do so. Depending on the goal, the investment strategy, and the available time for investing, different types of investors may each be correct, given their individual situations. However, individual success does not necessarily require the blanket exclusion of other investment options or techniques under all other circumstances.

For example, a young person who is putting aside money regularly for retirement will in all probability invest with long-term capital appreciation in mind, seeking to increase the amount of his or her retirement funds over time. A person who is looking for a run of small profits may engage in what is called day trading, where profits are measured in fractions of a dollar quickly gained. A person who is nearing retirement may reduce the number of more speculative stocks he or she owns and convert them to more conservative holdings. This person is giving up the chance for large gains in order to avoid untimely losses. Someone who has retired may be looking for a reliable income stream to support his or her desired lifestyle. The retiree will sell some stocks previously held for appreciation and invest the proceeds in stocks paying steady dividends or high-grade bonds with safe interest payments.

Given their divergent goals, does it make any sense for the young day trader to criticize the dividend strategy of the retiree? Should the technical analyst seeking to predict the projected movement of a stock over the next several days scoff at the multiyear strategy of the long-term value investor? I think not.

For most individuals, investing is a two-step process. So far most of our attention has been directed toward the first step, the purchase of a stock. We will now briefly look at the second step, the sale of that stock.

7

Selling

One of Albert Einstein's more famous quotes dealt with finance, not physics. He said, "Compound interest is the eighth wonder of the world. He who understands it earns it…He who doesn't…pays it."

Compound interest is interest that accrues on any previously unpaid interest as well as on the principal. In other words, interest on interest. Think of America's national debt. When one of its bonds comes due, the federal government may issue a new bond to raise the cash to pay off the principal and accrued interest on the old bond. The reverse is also true. Investment gains left to compound over a long time period can have amazing results. Many people have a hard time envisioning how compounding works. Perhaps the easiest way to understand it is to remember how you made a snowman as a child. You started with a snowball you could hold in your hand and kept rolling it around through the snow until you had a giant ball you could no longer push. Each time you rolled the ball it picked up more snow on its surface. As the surface grew, it picked up yet more snow over a larger area each time it moved.

Several financial authors over the years have demonstrated the results of starting to save early. One that might be of interest to grandparents is the one in which Gramma and Grampa open an IRA for their grandchild on his or her 18th birthday with a $2,000 deposit. They put the same amount into the account on the each of the next three birthdays and then stop. If the IRA is left untouched until the grandchild reaches the age of 65, the balance could exceed one million dollars, depending on the average rate of return over the forty-four year period. Now, that would be quite a legacy.

To determine your investment returns, you can use the mathematical rule of seventy-two. It states that you can determine your annual rate of return on an investment if you know how many years it takes for the investment to double. If you divide the number seventy-two by the number of years, the result is the annual rate of return (as a whole number). Conversely, if you know your rate of return on the investment, you can determine how long it will take for your investment to double. Using the same formula, you divide seventy-two by your annual rate of return (as a whole number), and the result is the approximate number of years it will take for the investment to double.

PARTING IS SUCH SWEET SORROW

Most investment books concentrate on the process of buying stocks. The when and why of selling are usually just afterthoughts. The foundation for selling is really a question of the holding period for your investment. Warren Buffett apparently does not have this issue since his holding period can be "forever." Those of us without a stock portfolio in the billions are not so lucky. Actually, as SEC filings reveal, even Buffett sells on occasion. The time horizon for day traders can be short, with buying and selling happening in rapid succession. Trader Jesse Livermore outlined his selling philosophy in his book *How to Trade in Stocks*: "To put this in another way I have two stops in mind when I enter a trade. I have a 'PRICE STOP' and I have a 'TIME STOP.' I will not stay with any trade more than a few points if it moves against me and I will not stay with a stock position for more than a few days if the stock does not perform as I expect it to perform."[1]

So, you have a stock holding spectrum starting with "forever" and diminishing to "a few days." What is an investor to do?

The main character in *Reminiscences of a Stock Operator* (based on Livermore) discussed his experiences as an early trader and then later on, when he had determined how to really profit from his decisions. He explained:

> I made up my mind to be wise and play carefully, conservatively. Everybody knew that the way to do that was to take profits and buy back your stocks on reactions. And that is precisely what I did, or rather what I tried to do; for I often took profits and waited for a reaction that never came. And I saw my stock go kiting up ten points more and I am sitting there with my four-point profit safe in my conservative pocket. They say you never grow poor taking profits. No, you don't. But neither do you grow rich taking a four-point profit in a bull market. I think I took a long step forward in my trading education when I realized at last that when old Mr. Partridge kept on telling the other customers, "Well, you know this is a bull market." he really meant to tell them that the big money was not in the individual fluctuations but in the main movements—that is, not in reading the tape but in sizing up the entire market and its trend.
>
> That is about all I learned—to study general conditions, to take a position and stick to it. In a bull market your game is to buy and hold until you believe that the bull market is near its end. To do this you must study general conditions and not tips or special factors affecting individual stocks. Then get out of all your stocks; get out for keeps![2]

As stated above, one of the oldest Wall Street proverbs is "you never go broke taking profits." For some people one of the frustrating features of selling a stock is then watching its price continue to rise. This is the result of forgetting why they sold in the first place. It seems a lot like paying any attention to the remarriage of an ex-spouse. Why should they care? The reason for the divorce still remains, and that should be the end of it.

If you buy a stock because it fits your investment strategy and hold it long enough, as Al Frank suggests, it should increase in price if your strategy is a good one. As we have learned, patience is a very important part of investing. Give the stock time to perform. Assuming a price increase, there are three reasons to sell.

First, if the stock has increased in price to the point that it represents an oversized percentage of your portfolio, you need to sell enough to get the shares' percentage back to the level that meets your diversification strategy. This could be 5 percent or whatever maximum percentage of your total portfolio you have decided an individual stock can represent. Assuming the stock still meets your investment standards, you simply sell enough to rebalance your account. You do not want to own so much of a company's stock that a large drop in share price will do significant damage to your overall portfolio.

Second, the stock price rises to the point you feel it is too expensive to continue to hold. If you buy a stock with a low P/E ratio, the price may have risen to the point that the P/E is higher than the level at which you typically buy. As an example, let's assume you buy one hundred shares of a stock for thirty dollars per share with a P/E ratio of ten. As you know, this means that the company is earning three dollars per share. Time passes, and the company is now earning five dollars per share. The market has noticed the earnings increase, and investors now want to own the stock. With this increased interest, the shares now trade at one hundred dollars per share with a P/E of twenty. Your initial investment of $3,000 has now grown to $10,000. If you feel the stock is now at a level that you would not buy it, you could sell all or a portion of your holdings (remembering your diversification percentages) and reinvest the money in another low-P/E stock.

Third, if you are a new investor building your portfolio one stock at a time, you will obviously need to diversify over time. That first stock you buy represents 100 percent of your portfolio. You need to buy other stocks. There is an interesting mathematical formula that helps with this task. As an example, let's assume you purchased one hundred shares of a stock for thirty dollars per share for a total investment of $3,000. The stock is now trading at forty dollars per share. If you sell seventy-five shares at forty dollars per share, you recoup your initial investment of $3000, and you still own twenty-five shares. A sale of 75 percent of the shares of a stock after the price has increased by a third allows you to continue to hold the stock with no remaining personal funds invested. You take your money and buy another stock. This formula works regardless of the number of shares you buy and the initial price you pay.

If the stock has not performed well in your time frame for owning it, be that three years or three hours, you might sell it and move on. You may have picked the stock for all the right reasons, but the investment may still not be successful. Be ready to accept losses; they happen even to the best investors. Conventional wisdom holds that you never hang onto a losing stock with the hope of getting back to even. You are missing too many other opportunities. You should take your money out of the loser and reinvest in a potential winner.

Conversely, although the stock is performing poorly, if it still meets your investment criteria and you view it as a long-term investment, you might continue to hold it. Yes, that is the exact opposite of the previously mentioned rule, but the qualifier is *long-term investment*. You must remember why you bought the stock in the first place. Indeed, you might actually consider buying more at the cheaper price. No one ever said investing was going to be easy.

8

The Computer—Time Bomb or
Investment Tool?

FROM ESSAYS TO EQUATIONS

One of the earliest and most enduring books on economics, *An Inquiry into the Nature and Causes of the Wealth of Nations*, was written by the real Adam Smith and published in 1776. A Scot educated as a moral philosopher, Smith took ten years to research and write his classic. Referred to popularly as *The Wealth of Nations*, many consider the treatise to be the foundation of many modern economic theories. The 1,200-page book contains several tables of goods and their prices in Smith's day, but unlike many books on economics today, *Wealth of Nations* contains no mathematical equations to demonstrate the movement of money through a country's economy.

Possibly the most studied and documented event in the history of Wall Street is the October 1929 market crash. It is the standard by which all other US market meltdowns continue to be measured. In my opinion, the best and certainly the most entertaining analysis of this event is Professor John Kenneth Galbraith's work *The Great Crash 1929*. It was first published in 1955 and has remained in print ever since. Galbraith, a professor for many years at Harvard, attributed the long-running success of *The Great Crash* to the fact that every time sales of the book would slip to the point of going out of print, there would be another market bubble and subsequent drop, which would rekindle public interest in the financial devastation of 1929. With humor and insight, Galbraith laid out the events in America during the roaring '20s and their tumultuous conclusion. Galbraith, like the first Adam Smith, used prose, not mathematics, to explain economic events.

The second Adam Smith of *The Money Game* fame discussed economists in one of his other books, *Paper Money*. He pointed out the transition to economic mathematics as follows:

> There were once two kinds of economists, one might argue: the Smiths and the Ricardos. The Smith is the 1723 Adam Smith and the Ricardo is David Ricardo, his immediate successor. Both the Smiths and the Ricardos were concerned with human activity and with the institutions that produce, preserve and distribute wealth. The Smiths observed; the Ricardos sought the universal and logical principles, using algebra and its succeeding languages.
>
> Today the Ricardos are fashionable and the Smiths are not. Economists who write well in English—there may be eight of them—run the risk of being labeled with the pejorative term "literary." The Ricardos admire the elegance of perfect equations; the highest terms of their praise are "rigorous" and "scientific."[1]

Another financial author known for writing ability, not equations, is Peter L. Bernstein. In 1992 he wrote *Capital Ideas—The Improbable Origins of Modern Wall Street*. In this work he chronicled the evolution of modern investment theories. Starting with Louis Bachelier's 1900 doctoral dissertation, *The Theory of Speculation*, Bernstein traced the evolution of Bachelier's dissertation with its formulas, which was rediscovered by later economists about sixty years after its publication.

Bachelier's ideas were transformed into the modern portfolio theory (MPT). Using MPT and its supporting mathematical equations, investment professionals assemble portfolios of assets to either maximize return at a certain level of risk or minimize risk while achieving a desired rate of return. It should come as no surprise that the use of equations in financial investing came at the same time as computers capable of executing those complex equations became the financial weapons of choice on Wall Street. Bernstein summarized investment by equation as follows:

> There is Louis Bachelier in 1900, holed up in the Sorbonne scratching out eternal verities about the behavior of speculative markets…Fischer Black, Myron Scholes, and Robert Merton change the whole world of finance by staring at differential equations. Through it all, the only sound we hear is the clanking of primitive computers…The clatter of the computer and the roar of the trading floor are the sounds of a great battle in which investors compete with one another to determine who can buy at the lowest and sell at the highest.[2]

One of a growing number of critics of formulaic financial theories is the Wall Street veteran and author Nassim Nicholas Taleb. In his 2004 best seller, *Fooled by Randomness—The Hidden Role of Chance in Life and in the Markets*, Taleb takes economists to task for their reliance on equations. He points out that using mathematics does not necessarily make economics a hard science but rather leads to problems. He wrote, "Indeed the mathematics they dealt with did not work in the real world, possibly because we needed richer classes of processes—and they refused to accept the fact that no mathematics at all was probably better."[3]

Criticism of computerized, equation-driven investing has grown in the public media after several highly publicized investment disasters.

THE COMPUTER: TIME BOMB

Earlier we followed a trading strategy attributed to Jesse Livermore, the famous trader of the 1920s. Back then Livermore's tools consisted of the telephone and the ticker tape, which allowed him to follow the changes in price with the shortest delay. In today's fast-paced trading, most on Wall Street use computers to initiate, follow, and close out their trades. They also use computer programs to run the trades. When they buy stocks, some individual investors and traders will also instruct their brokers or program their computers to sell the stocks if the price drops by a preset amount (say 5 percent of the purchase price). This instruction is called a stop loss order. The stop loss order can also be used to lock in a gain. If the stock has increased in price, the individual may, at any time, set a price below the current market price at which the stock is to be sold, thereby locking in the amount of gain the person is hoping to make without having to constantly monitor the market. As the price increases, the stop loss order price can be raised. This is one fairly basic strategy that can be initiated from the individual's computer (or with a phone call to the broker). On its face this sounds like a smart, conservative approach to investing and trading. The individual has quantified and limited any loss while letting any profits run. If used on a grand scale, however, unintended consequences can result.

The federal government appointed the Brady Commission to report on the October 1987 market crash when the Dow Jones Industrial Average dropped 508 points (22.6 percent) in one day. The commission concluded the following:

> The precipitous market decline of mid-October was "triggered" by specific events: an unexpectedly high merchandise trade deficit which pushed interest rates to new high levels, and proposed tax legislation which led to the collapse of stocks of a number of takeover candidates. This initial decline ignited

mechanical, price-insensitive selling by a number of institutions employing portfolio insurance strategies and a small number of mutual fund groups reacting to redemptions. The selling by these investors, and the prospect of further selling by them, encouraged a number of aggressive trading-oriented institutions to sell in anticipation of further market declines. This selling, in turn, stimulated further reactive selling by portfolio insurers and mutual funds.[4]

In his book *Irrational Exuberance*, Professor and Nobel Laureate Robert J. Shiller summarized the Brady report as follows: "By 'price-insensitive selling' they mean selling that comes in response to a price drop but is insensitive to how low the price goes before the sale is concluded—selling at any price. The Brady Commission was saying, in effect, that the crash of 1987 was a negative bubble."[5]

Portfolio insurance was the name of the computer program that instructed the investors' computers to sell stocks when they had declined by a certain amount—in effect a stop loss order. The problem was that many different computers' selling programs kicked in at the same time, leading to ever-lower prices and repeated sell orders, over and over, in October 1987. This appears remarkably similar to the avalanche of margin calls leading to the vicious cycle of ever-lower prices and repeated margin calls in October 1929. In his book *Capital Ideas—The Improbable Origins of Modern Wall Street* Peter Bernstein pointed out that the portfolio insurance programs were based on the assumption there would be buyers when it came time to sell. As the selling increased, potential buyers moved to the sidelines. It became very apparent that not many people will try to catch a sharp knife as it is tumbling to the ground.

A new form of computer trading started on Wall Street several years ago, and the financial press has reported some of its more spectacular effects. There are firms, referred to as high frequency traders

(HFT), that program their computers with complicated algorithms to identify small profit opportunities in the market. These traders make thousands of trades in rapid succession within seconds. Some trades are completed, and others are cancelled. Although the actual profit per trade is small, the huge volume of trading can result in overall gains. It has been reported that in the past, as much as two-thirds of daily trading volume on some stock, options, and futures exchanges is the result of the computer trading programs employed by such firms. Much of this trading occurs on electronic trading exchanges, which are separate from the more established exchanges used by individual investors and their brokers, but trades on one exchange are monitored by traders on all exchanges and can have a spillover effect on prices on other exchanges.

Although the true causes may never be agreed upon, the HFT firms are alleged to have played a role in the May 6, 2010 Flash Crash, during which the Dow Jones Industrial Average fell almost one thousand points and then recovered most of that decline in a matter of minutes. A joint report by the US Securities and Exchange Commission and the Commodity Futures Trading Commission, agencies that investigated the event, indicated that May 6 was "unusually turbulent," with a widely negative trend. In the afternoon a mutual fund was trying to sell a large number of S&P 500 futures contracts to hedge its other equity positions. Several HFT traders began buying them and then quickly reselling them to other HFT firms. This buying and selling picked up steam, resulting in what was termed a "hot potato" effect on exceptionally large volume. The result of this repeated back-and-forth trading sent the price of the particular contract down 4 percent in about four minutes. This precipitous drop spilled over into the equity markets, and the price of an S&P 500 ETF also plunged. These movements triggered many computer stop loss programs that paid no heed to price levels; the computers simply followed orders. It was reported that some large companies, like Proctor & Gamble, traded as low as one penny a share at one point.

The Flash Crash is one example of computers run amok affecting the entire market. Sometimes the damage is isolated and wreaks havoc only on the HFT running the computer program. The poster child for this sort of self-inflicted financial wound is Knight Capital Group. Knight Capital was a Wall Street trading firm that, on August 1, 2012, was rolling out a new computer program designed to give it an advantage in the world of HFT traders. The new software started at the opening of the New York Stock Exchange and, in the forty-five minutes before the NYSE closed down Knight's trading, resulted in trades that cost Knight Capital approximately $440 million in losses. The stock of publicly traded Knight Capital Group dropped a combined 95 percent in two days. Without a quick bailout from other Wall Street firms, the company would have ended up in bankruptcy. Investigations confirmed that the damage was caused by a bug in the new software, which obviously had not been tested enough before being put into action. What was left of Knight Capital was acquired by another investment company in December 2012.

One of the largest financial disasters that can be traced to computer trading was the collapse of the hedge fund Long-Term Capital Management (LTCM). LTCM was organized in February 1994 with a $1.25 billion equity base, raised from wealthy investors and financial institutions by a group of Wall Street professionals and several Nobel Laureate economists. These disparate individuals combined to create a computer trading and hedging program that focused on the differences, or spreads, between interest rates on various types of bonds. Two famous economists, Robert C. Merton of Harvard and Myron S. Scholes, one of the developers of the Black-Scholes model for pricing options, were initial partners in LTCM. They were proponents of the efficient market hypothesis, popularly called the random walk theory.

The fund's initial investment strategy was based on the theory that any unusual spreads between the interest rates of different bonds would, in a rational and efficient market, ultimately narrow and converge. The company's computers were programmed to seek out and identify these spreads, which allowed LTCM to take market positions in the bonds that would be profitable if and when those spreads narrowed as predicted. When LTCM started, it was the only market player investing in such a way, which resulted in its spectacular early success. Based on that success, LTCM was able to borrow billions of dollars from large banks in order to make its investments on margin. Its early annual returns on equity were astronomical (28 percent in its first year of operation and 59 percent in 1995 before fees). Such returns led to more money coming in from investors and more money made available from lenders—a sort of virtuous circle.

There is an old saying that "Imitation is the best form of flattery." As is so often the case, LTCM's success on Wall Street attracted attention and led other market professionals and their companies to figure out and copy LTCM's profitable trading strategy. Soon there were many funds and traders playing LTCM's game. With the new competition, it was more difficult for LTCM to establish positions and make profits from the spreads. As a result LTCM started to trade other financial assets, hoping to garner the same profits as in the past, including an asset called equity volatility (which is too complicated for me to understand other than to say it was a naked bet, not an investment).

Unfortunately, expanding its trading horizons was not the answer. One of these new trades by LTCM was in Russian bonds. They believed that Russia would be able to pay its bonds, a belief they held right up to August 17, 1998, when the Russian government announced a debt moratorium and defaulted on its bonds. At this point, to make matters worse, Russia also devalued its currency, the ruble, which LTCM had also bet would not happen. During this time of market turmoil, almost all the other trades LTCM had set in place turned against them. Since LTCM had used so much leverage (margin loans at a ratio of twenty-eight dollars of debt to every one dollar of equity in 1997), its losses were staggering. It all came to a grinding halt for LTCM in August 1998. Bond spreads had increased to levels never seen before, much wider than the computers at LTCM had been programmed to anticipate. LTCM lost $1.9 billion of its capital in one month. Its remaining capital, $2.8 billion, was dwarfed by its $125 billion of assets supported by debt. These numbers do not include the other LTCM positions in derivatives and swap spreads, which added to its unsustainable debt load. To make matters worse, the loans that had been so freely extended early on were being called, and finding new loans became impossible, all at the worst possible moment for the fund.

There is a hard truth about lending money. If you lend someone $1,000, you are a creditor; however, if you lend someone $100 million, you are a partner. As LTCM moved ever closer to the bankruptcy cliff, it became apparent to everyone on Wall Street and in the Federal Reserve that a collapse of LTCM would have devastating effects upon the financial system, not only in the United States but around the world. It had so many outstanding trades with so many other institutions that its failure could conceivably cause worldwide damage. The Federal Reserve brought together the biggest investment firms on Wall Street and LTCM's lenders in emergency meetings over several days to address the problems. The Fed forged an agreement that, with other countries, would provide $3.65 billion in equity to LTCM. This amount, plus its remaining $400 million in equity, provided the fund with the needed capital to remain in existence until its trades could be unwound and it could be liquidated in an orderly fashion.

The entire saga of LTCM is told in remarkable detail by Roger Lowenstein in his 2000 book *The Rise and Fall of Long-Term Capital Management, When Genius Failed*. In summing up the little over four-year run of LTCM with its arcane computer modeling and efficient market philosophy, Lowenstein said it best:

Reared on Merton's and Scholes' teachings of efficient markets, the professors actually believed that prices would go and go directly where the models said they should. The professors' conceit was to think that models could forecast the limits of behavior. In fact, the models could tell them what was reasonable or what was predictable based on the past. The professors overlooked the fact that people, traders included, are not always reasonable. This is the true lesson of Long-Term's demise. No matter what the models say, traders are not machines guided by silicon chips; they are impressionable and imitative; they run in flocks and retreat in hordes.

The next time a Merton proposes an elegant model to manage risks and foretell odds, the next time a computer with a perfect memory of the past is said to quantify risks in the future, investors should run—and quickly—the other way.[6]

MARKETS AND BIRDS OF A DIFFERENT FEATHER

Dr. Nassim Nicholas Taleb has been described as "part literary essayist, part empiricist and part no-nonsense mathematical trader." He is most famous for his books, *Fooled by Randomness, The Hidden Role of Chance in Life and in the Markets*, published in 2004, and *The Black Swan, The Impact of the Highly Improbable*, published in 2007. Both books take on conventional financial theory.

In his prologue to *Fooled by Randomness*, Dr. Taleb explains that his book is about luck, which is mistakenly perceived by those lucky souls as evidence of their personal skills, and about randomness, which is mistakenly seen as a surprising event that might have been, but was not, anticipated. Something unusual (good or bad) happens in the market, shocking everyone, and financial reporters immediately offer explanations. "We don't know why" is an unacceptable answer in the public media. That would make for a fairly short television broadcast or newspaper story with a concomitant loss of advertising dollars.

Taleb criticizes economists, journalists, television analysts, and others for refusing to acknowledge that the one-in-ten-billion (or higher) possibility really can happen. Their statistical analyses, Gaussian distribution (standard bell curve) charts, and computer programs do not take such extremely rare probabilities into account. Although they are armed with reams of data based on computer analyses of vast numbers of probabilities, Taleb believes they do not know what they do not know. Or, viewed more cynically, if they do know, they won't admit it.

All swans were thought to be white until in 1697 a Dutch explorer, Willem de Vlamingh, discovered a black one in Australia. One ugly bird destroyed a belief previously held by everyone in the ornithological world at that time. Dr. Taleb uses the term *black swan* to identify an event with three characteristics. First, the event is an outlier, which means it is beyond the expectations of most, if not all, people. It will not be revealed in a standard bell curve distribution. Second, it will have a significant effect or impact (think September 11, 2001 or the market crash of October 1987). Finally, it is an event in the wake of which people immediately demand an explanation. The question "How could this happen?" echoes down Wall Street.

The basic premise of *The Black Swan* is that events of this type actually happen with greater frequency than previously imagined. Black swans serve to remind us that we are not in total control—a terrifying thought for many. The implications of this for the stock market are significant. In his book Taleb provided two rates of return in a single graph. One line showed the return in the US stock market over the past fifty years. The second one charted the return without the ten most volatile days (up or down) over that same fifty-year period. The reduction in return without those ten days is dramatic.

Taleb describes his trading philosophy as one in which he limits his losses and leaves open the possibility of large gains if and when an unusual event should take place. He compliments traders who buy options, which means a loss is limited to the option fee paid but which provide the trader with the opportunity to reap an outsized profit if something unexpected were to occur. His investment strategy was always to look for a black swan even though he was not sure in what form it might appear.

He pointed out the dangers of inductive reasoning noted by the philosopher Bertrand Russell. Inductive reasoning begins with observations that generate inferences, then perceived patterns that lead ultimately to theories to address an issue or problem. Echoing Russell, Dr. Taleb described the dangers of inductive reasoning from the perspective of a turkey. The bird considers its human caretakers to be friends who provide shelter, water, and food on a daily basis until the fourth Wednesday of November, when something hitherto unimaginable happens. For the turkey, past experience counts for naught on that fateful day.

I heard a story that illustrates the same point.

A woman inherited some stock in her local bank when her husband died. The local bank was purchased by a larger bank in the area, which in turn was purchased by a regional bank, which was itself purchased by a national financial organization. With stock splits, several subsequent bank mergers, and a steadily rising price for the shares in the larger, merged, publicly traded financial institutions along the way, she had accumulated a substantial number of shares worth a great deal of money. The bank stock became a significant percentage of her portfolio. If she sold the stock, the tax bill would be significant, so she decided to hang on to her shares and let the profits ride (one of investing's golden rules). Things went well until the day the financial institution failed due to "accounting irregularities." The market price of her shares dropped to less than a dollar per share within days of the public announcement that the management had been cooking the books for years. Not the first time such a thing has happened in the market but certainly for her a black swan.

Taleb's message to you is to at least consider the possible damage if the truly unthinkable event, outside of a computer's programming or your imagination, were actually to happen.

SO MANY STOCKS, SO LITTLE TIME

If an individual investor decides to put together a portfolio based on value investing, the previously mentioned books can provide the strategy and rules for analyzing stocks that meet the investor's requirements. To continue the gold miner analogy, the value investor will need the necessary information to separate real nuggets from fool's gold. The remaining question is how to find useful data.

In the bad "good old days," the individual investor had to almost take on a second job—the job of a securities analyst, poring over scores of company communications, balance sheets, income statements, and the like. Since this is a full-time job for the analysts on Wall Street, the individual investor would be faced with the almost impossible task of finding the time in his or her busy life to devote to identifying companies that could prove to be good investments.

Several biographies of Warren Buffett report that for most of his life, he has devoted substantially all of his waking moments to stock analysis. Apparently his family understood or at least put up with his single-minded devotion to finding good stocks. Given his financial success, it obviously paid off. Not many individual investors will be able to convince their spouses that they can give up their day jobs because they will be able to do the same. If faced with such a proposal, most spouses would probably suggest their partners go into psychological analysis, not financial.

There are almost 5,300 companies traded on the NYSE (New York Stock Exchange) and the NASDAQ (the exchange formerly known as the National Association of Securities Dealers Automated Quotations). The total universe of stocks increases significantly if you include the stocks traded on exchanges affiliated with the NYSE and all other exchanges around the world. Reviewing all of the available information on all of these companies would be a daunting task, even for a full-time Wall Street analyst. Many analysts specialize in one or two industries, greatly reducing the number of companies they must follow.

Before computers, analysts and individual investors had to plod through volumes of material to find attractive candidates for purchase. One method was to review the monthly *Standard & Poor's [S&P] Stock Guide*, a small, thick pamphlet with financial information printed in very small type for all traded stocks. An analyst or an individual investor could spend hours combing through the lists of statistics for each company, looking for a stock that met some or all of his or her financial metrics. As the computer took over Wall Street, this arduous task was performed by computerized stock screeners that quickly identified stocks with the analyst's desired financial ratios. The computer accomplished in seconds what had previously taken many hours.

The computer has changed the landscape of stock analysis. Instead of the drudgery of searching through reams of printed information, an investor can create computerized stock screeners to identify companies that meet his or her requirements. Most if not all brokerage companies with an online presence provide their customers with this time-saving tool at no charge.

If, for example, the investor wants a list of companies traded on the New York Stock Exchange with market capitalization of $2 billion or more; annual earnings growth of not less than 15 percent; paying a dividend of not less than 2 percent per annum; and trading at a price/ earnings ratio of not more than fifteen, then the investor enters these requirements, and the screener will find all publicly traded companies that meet them. Value, growth, and contrarian investors can adjust the screening requirements to fit their particular investment strategies and press the "enter" button for the results. In seconds a list of investment candidates appears on the screen.

In setting up the screener, the investor can establish the stock exchanges to be searched: the NYSE, the American Stock Exchange (AMEX), the NASDAQ, and the over the counter market (OTC) or all of them. If the investor were to choose all of them, the universe of stocks to be screened would include over seven thousand companies. The level of market capitalization (stock price multiplied by number of traded shares) can be established. The investor can limit the screener to companies in a particular industry. The screening tool can search for companies paying dividends with specific yields or trading at certain price limits.

A screener can be programmed to search for companies with preset analysts' ratings. The investor can set the screener to look for companies with histories (up to five years) of desired revenue and earnings growth rates or with analysts' revenue and earnings estimates going forward. If the investor wants to focus on price, various standards can be established, including the price performance of a company when compared to its industry or to the S&P 500 index.

Valuation ratios can be established, such as price/earnings, price/book, or price/sales. Of particular importance to investors looking for dividends would be the dividend payout ratio. This ratio measures what percentage of a company's earnings are paid out annually to shareholders in dividends. The lower the ratio, the better the chances that the company should not have to reduce or suspend its dividend payments in the future. The screener can be set for various tests of financial strength, such as ratios for debt to equity, return on equity, quick and current ratios, and cash flow per share, to name just a few. There are also various settings for technical measures of a company. Essentially, stock screening is a process of elimination. With each new metric you add, the number of companies meeting your requirements is reduced.

By way of example, I will set up a stock screener offered by an online brokerage company on my home computer and report how it winnows the number of stocks available in the market down to stocks I might want to research further. I will use the typically offered stock screener metrics. The different criteria I set will be identified in bold.

I will start by selecting the stock exchanges I want to search. Under **basic criteria** I will choose the NYSE, the AMEX, the NASDAQ, and the OTC market. That results in a total of 7,029 stocks.

I want companies tracked by Wall Street, since it is hard to make money on a stock if nobody has heard about it. It helps if analysts follow a company and bring it to the attention of the investing public. I will add **analyst ratings**, specifically the Standard & Poor's [S&P] Earnings and Dividend Rankings. I want to see companies rated from B to A+ by S&P. I pick this range of ratings solely for purposes of example. An individual investor must decide what, if any, rating level to use in limiting his or her search. This reduces the number of stocks to 1,417 companies meeting just these two requirements. Similarly, I will select **analyst coverage** and set it at a minimum of five analysts covering the companies. This reduces our group of companies to 897. At this point the screen is not identifying specific companies, just the number meeting the three criteria I have set so far.

Now I look at **company performance**. I set two categories in this section: revenue growth history for the past five years and earnings growth history for the same period. I choose a minimum of an annual 15 percent growth rate. A revenue growth history of 15 percent or better lowers the number of companies to 193, and a similar requirement for earnings growth history drops the number to 103. As you can see, the number of companies has dropped significantly with each added financial metric.

The next category is **price performance**. Since I am just trying to narrow the field of companies to look at, I am not going to pay any attention to price at this point. If price is a factor, I can look at that once I have my list of companies. Therefore, I do not select anything from this section.

The sixth general criteria is **valuation**. Here is where we can pick companies with the ratios discussed in the books on fundamental analysis. To keep things simple, I am going to select only one: the price/earnings ratio for the trailing twelve months (TTM). I will set it at twenty or below. This reduces our field of stocks to seventy-two.

I further limit my search based on **financial strength**. This field includes quite a number of criteria, but again I am going to choose only one: a return on equity of 20 percent or better. The resulting number is now down to sixty-four companies meeting all of the measures I have established so far.

The final section is **technicals**, but since we are approaching this exercise as a fundamental analyst might, I will skip this section.

My final step is to hit the "view matches" button. The stock screener provides a list of the companies matching my criteria and specific criteria information for each company. How much easier can it get? Although the screeners provided by brokerage houses are very comprehensive, there are also basic stock screening programs available online you can access at no charge. If you want to experiment constructing your own screen, you could go to www. Google.com/finance/stockscreener.

STOCK SCREENERS AND STOCK RESEARCH

When we completed our stock screening, we were left with sixty-four possible investments. Since the screener was pretty basic and for illustration purposes only, we won't bother looking at the companies with these rudimentary financial characteristics. On the other hand, it is worth exploring the next step an individual investor must take in order to find the investment candidates to consider in making his or her final buying decision. The computer saved us quite a bit of time, but now we must spend some study time.

Many investment and brokerage companies produce stock market and individual stock research; however, their reports are not free to the public. S&P and Value Line are two well-known US research companies. Although their websites provide information and commentary, an investor must subscribe in order to receive stock reports. Such research companies sell their reports to individual investors and to stock brokerage companies. In order to access them at no charge, the individual investor must establish an account with a brokerage firm. Obviously this is not a large hurdle, since the investor has to do this anyway in order to place buy and sell orders in the market.

I think the individual investor who has decided to handle his or her investments is best served by opening his or her account with an online broker in order to save trading fees and expenses. Most of them have fixed trade fees, which are usually less than ten dollars per transaction. Some of the well-known US online companies are Charles Schwab, E*TRADE, TD Ameritrade, and Scottrade.

All of these online firms have links on their websites that will send the investor to their research tools. Those tools include stock screeners; third-party stock reports, such as those published by Standard & Poor's; and research reports provided by the broker. I have not seen the Value Line reports offered by any brokerage firm I have used; however, they are available at most public libraries. For no cost the investor can set up a stock screener with the investor's requirements and then review reports on the matching companies identified on the screen, all without leaving the broker's website.

STOCKS AND USED CARS

Awhile ago I had a discussion about stocks with one of my daughters. I identified a few companies that were then paying decent dividends with a 3 percent rate of return. I was surprised when she said she would not buy a couple of the stocks I mentioned because she did not want to support those businesses. She thought she would be buying the stock directly from the companies, thereby giving them her money for use in a business she did not condone.

I explained that unless she purchased a stock in a company's public offering, she was buying from another investor, and the transaction had no effect on the company's business in any way. Stocks are like used cars. A car manufacturer makes no money when someone buys one of its used models from a dealer or a private party. This raises a good point.

Most used-car purchasers now ask for the Carfax® reports on the vehicles they are considering. In addition there is a wealth of knowledge about car models available online. Thankfully the days of walking onto a car lot and blindly picking out a vehicle based on little more than the color and a salesman's persuasive patter are long since over. A stock purchaser can and should do the same. He or she should check out the company before buying its shares.

There are several well-respected sources of financial information on companies and their stocks. One of the most widely known is the Standard & Poor's Report. An S&P report on a company contains several pages of information about the company's industry, the business and financial state of the company (including most of the financial metrics Ben Graham looked for), and other important information a value investor would want before committing to a purchase.

S&P'S TAKE ON COCA-COLA

To start, I need to make an important point. In no way am I recommending Coca-Cola as an investment opportunity or a good stock to buy. I picked this company because it is a globally recognized brand. Also, I imagine everyone has had a Coke at one time or another.

With that disclaimer out of the way, let's look at the August 27, 2011 Standard & Poor's report on The Coca Cola Co. (stock symbol: KO). I am going to give only a brief description of each page. I am not going to review the information in the report in detail.

Page one: The S&P recommendation (five star—strong buy), current price ($68.50 as of August 26), twelve-month target price ($79), and a description of KO's investment type (large-cap growth) are at the top of the page. The next section gives key stock statistics, such as the stock's fifty-two-week price range, its TTM earnings per share (EPS) of $5.37, the TTM price/earnings ratio (12.8), and additional information that would be of interest to the investor.

This page contains a price performance chart going back to 2008, which graphs what KO's stock has done over the last few years. These statistics are flanked by S&P's risk assessment, which shows that S&P considers the company relatively stable. Coke receives an evaluation of A+ and a relative strength Rank of strong. The highlights of the company and the investment rationale/risk prepared by the analyst—Esther Kwon, CFA—are located beneath the price performance chart. To the right of this analysis are revenue and earnings data going back to 2006. The section on dividend data for the previous four quarters is just below that. Quite a bit of information is provided on just this first page of the report. It would take an investor a lot of time to ferret out this data on his or her own.

Page two: This page contains the analyst's business summary. Next to this summary is corporate information, including the company's address, telephone number, executive officers, members of the board, and additional facts about the company.

Page Three: Here is the most sought-after information for the fundamental investor. At the top of the page are S&P's quantitative evaluations of the company, including its fair value rank and calculation for KO, the company's investability quotient percentile, volatility, technical evaluation, and insider activity. Next to this section is the expanded ratio analysis, which provides the price/sales ratio, the price/EBITDA ratio, the price/pretax income ratio, the price/earnings (P/E) ratio, and the average diluted shares outstanding for the years 2007 to 2010. An investor may consider one or more of these ratios significant in his or her personal investment strategy. It would take a good deal of time for an individual to determine them with a calculator.

The lower half of page three contains a large amount of data titled "company financials." This section includes per-share data, income statement analysis, balance sheet, and other financial figures for the past ten years. This is a treasure trove of information for the fundamental investor. The individual investor will find all of the data he or she may need in order to decide if Coke meets the investor's requirements for a good investment.

Page four: This page is devoted to the soft drink business, which is referred to as a subindustry of the consumer staples category of business. Analyst Esther Y. Kwon, CFA, discusses the soda business in her subindustry outlook. Accompanying her analysis is the stock performance for soft drinks, comparing it to consumer staples and the S&P 1500 Index, which shows month-end price performances of KO from 2007 through July 2011. Below this is data on Coke's peer group, which includes several Coca-Cola bottling companies, Dr. Pepper, PepsiCo, and others.

Page five: This page contains what is termed S&P analyst research notes and other company news, which includes reports and announcements about Coke going back to February 2011.

Page six: This page is devoted to reports on the way Coca Cola is viewed by the Wall Street analysts who cover the company. The page starts with a review of analysts' recommendations of buy, buy/hold, hold, weak hold, and sell going back to 2009. It lists the number of analysts covering Coke and its stock price. The page also contains the Wall Street consensus opinion of buy/hold and a list of the research companies in addition to S&P offering coverage of Coke. The page also includes Wall Street consensus Estimates for earnings for 2011 and 2012.

Page seven: On this page S&P provides a glossary of various financial measures contained in the previous pages, including S&P stars, S&P core earnings, its risk assessment, S&P quality rating, and more. This page describes S&P's proprietary modeling systems, such as the S&P fair value rank, fair value calculation, and investability quotient, among others.

Pages eight, nine, and ten: these pages contain what could be called the fine print—S&P's disclosures and disclaimers concerning its report on Coke.

If you are a fundamental investor, you will find in this report most if not all of the investment data and financial statistics on The Coca-Cola Co. you might need in order to analyze the company. To make an investment in a stock without reviewing a report such as this is the equivalent of embarking on a cross-country car trip without maps or a GPS. The person ends up lost in either event.

If you want to dig deeper into a company, you can go to the Securities & Exchange Commission website called Edgar, where you can access the various reports the SEC requires publicly traded companies to file with it.

TRADING PLATFORMS AND SLOT MACHINES

One sure sign of a frothy market is the number and silliness of television commercials for online trading from brokerage firms. My all-time favorite is an ad aired in the late 1990s, during the dot-com bubble, that featured a plumber driving his truck to a job and talking about the island he had just purchased with the money he had made trading online. He attributed his success to the computerized trading tools offered by an online broker. It seems that as the market rockets upward, the ads increase proportionately, promising easy, quick profits. As with most advertising, this message should be taken with a grain (or shovel full) of salt.

Online brokers tout their trading platforms and low trading costs. The platforms offer computerized technical analysis with moving averages, volume and price charts, breaking news services, and whatever other indicators a trader might want to see on the screen. Some people make many small trades during the day and use leverage (margin loans) to increase profits. Given the costs, some of them probably give most of their profits and more back to the broker in interest charges and trading costs.

Different traders have different trading periods. Position or trend traders can hold their positions for several months to several years. The goal is to find a stock that is trending upward and hold on to it for the duration of the run. A second type of trading is called swing trading (a new name for momentum trading) with near-term time frames of several days to several weeks and intermediate terms of up to six months. The shortest time frame is the day trade, in which the trader holds a position for anywhere from several minutes up to a day. The day trader will usually close out all open positions at the end of the day to avoid losses he or she might otherwise incur if his or her positions remained exposed to the action of after-hours markets. Markets now follow the sun around the world; some market is open somewhere for trading every hour of the day.

The look of a trading screen is similar to that of a slot machine, with flashing lights and beeping sounds. I suspect the similarity is not coincidental. The gaming industry has spent a considerable amount of time and money determining what sort of display will keep a player feeding the machine. I believe online day trading on your home computer and playing the slots in a casino share many characteristics, not the least of which is that they are both, in essence, gambling.

The Securities & Exchange Commission has posted comments about day trading. Their advice included several statements, two of which I will share with you: "Be prepared to suffer severe financial losses. Day trading is an extremely stressful and expensive full-time job." Granted, these are from a regulatory agency, but they should give pause to the amateur trader interested in those supposedly easy and quick profits touted by the brokerage firms.

One advantage to slot machines—you need not pay a fee on top of your bet. Just drop in your money and play.

So far we have looked at equities. It is now time to look briefly at the much bigger market of debt instruments.

9

Debt Securities

WITH APOLOGIES TO SHAKESPEARE

I owe William Shakespeare an apology. In the play *Hamlet*, Polonius gives his son, Laertes, some fatherly advice as the young man leaves for school. He tells him, "Neither a borrower nor a lender be."[1] I had always attributed that line to Ben Franklin. In any event not many adhere to this proverb these days. From individuals to governments, the use of credit is ubiquitous. In April 2013 the US national debt exceeded $16 trillion. Total US debt, including household, corporate, and government borrowings, exceeded $50.7 trillion in 2009. According to the US Government Accountability Office, total **daily** trading volume in US bond markets in 2011 was $900 billion. You read that right: loans totaling $900 billion changed hands every day in America's 2011 debt markets. US Treasury debt made up $500 billion of that $900 billion total.

The types of debt are quite varied as well. There are US treasury securities; bonds issued by states, counties, and municipalities; US government agency debt; US corporate debt; secured and unsecured; as well as manufactured debt. Foreign bonds issued in US dollars for purchase by US citizens (called Yankee bonds) can also be found in US bond markets.

In addition to underwriting debt securities for public sale, Wall Street also manufactures debt securities. Investment banks will buy government and corporate bonds and combine them into a security called a collateralized debt obligation (CDO). They pool the debt and then divide it into what are called tranches, each with a different maturity, interest rate, and, in many instances, level of creditworthiness (the likelihood of repayment). *Tranche* is a French word for "slice." The investment bank marks up the price of the tranche to make its money and sells certificates for this new security to debt investors. Each portion of the pool of debt instruments is sold to someone looking for a particular cash flow and rate of return. These are pass-through securities in which the borrowers' repayments on the loans in the pool are recycled to make the payments to the CDO owners.

Some CDOs are made up of consumer debt. There are CDOs consisting of pools of credit card debt, student loans, or auto loans. Of recent infamy are mortgage-backed securities (MBS), also referred to as collateralized mortgage obligations (CMO). During the US real estate bubble in the early years of the twenty-first century, the mortgages taken out to finance the flood of home purchases found their way into CMOs distributed by Wall Street around the world. When the bubble burst and the recession hit, home values plummeted. Homeowners became either unable or unwilling to service the debt on their then much less valuable homes. In many instances the value of the home fell to less than the amount of mortgage debt on it. Homeowners in this situation are commonly referred to as being either upside down or underwater. As the homeowners' payments dried up, the CMOs containing those mortgages defaulted on a mammoth scale, and the debt market plunged into a credit crisis. Although probably not the only reason, worthless CMOs played a role in the recession of 2007 to 2009.

THE RISKS OF DEBT INVESTING

Ben Franklin summarized the dangers of lending in 1758 in *Poor Richard's Almanack* with his statement "Creditors have better memories than debtors."[2] Sometimes debtors just can't pay the money back. Individual debt investors face the same issue as global banks. How likely is repayment? This may be their primary concern, but there are other issues, not as obvious but just as important for individuals.

US Treasury obligations are considered the gold standard of debt. America has always repaid its loans. Notwithstanding recent congressional brinksmanship, most assume it always will. When financial markets in the world get rough, US Treasuries are seen as a safe haven by both individual and professional debt investors. Since repayment is not an issue, what other perils exist? Let's assume you buy a $10,000 US Treasury bond paying a rate of 8 percent per annum with a twenty-year maturity. If you hold that bond for twenty years, you will make 8 percent on your investment every year and get your principal back at maturity. Sounds pretty safe, doesn't it? However, under certain circumstances, you could face a loss of principal.

If you unexpectedly need cash and interest rates on similar treasuries have climbed to 10 percent in the market, you will not get the face value of your bond when you go to sell it. If the market rate is now 10 percent, why would anyone pay face value for your bond with an 8 percent yield? There are hundreds of billions of dollars of Treasuries traded every day, so it would not be hard for an investor to find that 10 percent yield. To get a 10 percent return on your 8 percent bond, the buyer will pay less than its face value such that your bond will yield 10 percent on the purchase price for him or her. If you must sell your Treasury, you will have lost some of your investment in the safest form of debt in the world because you needed immediate cash.

Let's look at the opposite and certainly more pleasant scenario. Assume interest rates have dropped since you bought your 8 percent bond. Now the going interest rate on similar bonds is 6 percent in the debt market. Since the money being generated on your bond exceeds the amount of money to be received at a market rate of 6 percent, you can now sell your Treasury for more than its face value in order to yield 6 percent to the buyer.

The risk for you, an individual bondholder, is twofold. First, can you hold the bond to maturity? Second, if you must sell, what has happened to interest rates in the interim? Market interest rates fluctuate daily, and you have no way of knowing what the rate might be if and when you need to sell.

It is said there are two constants in this life: death and taxes. I would suggest there is a third constant these days: inflation. The loaf of bread you bought a few years ago for two dollars now costs at least three dollars. The dollar you put away in a savings account ten years ago buys a lot less today. If you buy a 10 percent bond and inflation is running at 3 percent each year, inflation has reduced your real rate of return to 7 percent. Your real rate of return is then reduced even further by one of those other constants in life: taxes. If you lived through the years of high inflation in the late '70s and early '80s in the United States, you know how rampant inflation can impact investments. A 10 percent bond in an era of 12 percent inflation results in a loss of purchasing power at the rate of 2 percent every year, and the taxes you must pay on the interest you received will further deepen that loss. So, even the safest investment in the world, US debt, carries risk.

So, what is an individual investor to do?

Although stocks are viewed as riskier than debt instruments, they have generated annual returns of somewhere between 9 and 10 percent over many decades. If interest rates are high, in double digits, investors move into the debt market to garner these returns without the perceived risk of equities. When interest rates are at levels below the expected returns on stocks, investors gravitate back to the stock market.

I believe that in an era of low interest rates, an individual should view debt more as the place to put a portion of his or her money to keep it safe rather than as an investment with an interest return. To minimize the effect of interest rate fluctuations, the investor should stick to short-term debt obligations—that is, maturities of several months up to not more than two or three years. Long-term obligations (ten to thirty-year terms) are the ones whose values are most impacted by interest rate moves. Many people liken the stock market to a casino. There are very few big, long-term winners in either. As Kenny Rogers sang in his hit song "The Gambler," "You never count your money when you're sitting at the table."[3] When the stock market is on a roll and your equities are soaring, it is counterintuitive to sell some of that stock. However, if you want to keep those gains, take some of the chips off the table. You should put some of those profits in a place where, as my father used to say, "Wall Street can't get it."

Savings accounts and certificates of deposit in federally insured institutions and short-term US Treasuries (maturities of less than a year) are dull, pedestrian investments, but they provide the individual investor with places to put money with little risk of principal loss. The fact that the money is safe from equity market risk can be seen as more important than the yield made on the debt. If an individual investor wants to buy US Treasuries without incurring a brokerage fee or commission, he or she can buy online from the US Treasury at www.treasurydirect.gov.

IF THE COOK LEAVES FOR LUNCH

A cook who is paid for quantity, not quality, and does not have to eat his own cooking will probably not follow the recipe all that carefully. A mortgage lender in the same position will have little concern for the credit quality of the loans being booked. This was the situation during the last years of the US housing bubble of 2001 through 2005.

Anyone who has seen Frank Capra's 1946 Christmas classic *It's a Wonderful Life* knows how a bank operates. Back then, if a person wanted to buy a house, he or she would go to the lending institution and apply for a mortgage loan. The banker would carefully check the applicant's credit rating, job history, and stability; get an appraisal of the property; and decide whether to make the loan. The bank recycled one person's savings into another person's home loan and made money on the interest-rate spread. The bank had to be conservative in its lending practices, since it still had to meet the daily withdrawals of its customers regardless of a borrower's repayment of a loan.

In 1938, late in the Depression, the US government established the Federal National Mortgage Association to stimulate the moribund economy and encourage home ownership by issuing bonds and using the money to buy mortgages from lenders, thereby providing lenders with more money and making it easier for people to get a home mortgage. Adam Smith explained Fannie Mae and its relatives in his book *Paper Money*:

> The Great Society produced a Second Wave of housing legislation, more agencies, more acronyms, this time with some endearing nicknames. FNMA or "Fannie Mae," the Federal National Mortgage Association, was already in existence... Now Fannie Mae had a little sister, "Ginnie Mae," GNMA, the Government National Mortgage Association. Ginnie Mae could buy mortgages that Fannie Mae couldn't, because Ginnie Mae's were for subsidized housing. And there was a little brother, "Freddie Mac," the Federal Home Loan Mortgage Corporation. Like his sisters, Freddie could raise money by selling bonds in the public marketplace; unlike his sisters, who could keep the mortgages, Freddie Mac bought mortgages from savings and loans when they needed cash and sold them back when they were flush.[4]

Wall Street copied the Fannie/Ginnie/Freddie models and got into the mortgage-backed securities game during the housing bubble years in a big way. Earlier, Congress had passed laws to make home loans afford-able for many people whose credit was not strong enough to qualify them for regular home loans. These were referred to as subprime mort-gage loans. As the housing bubble picked up speed, subprime mortgages were offered by mortgage brokers with very low teaser rates of interest for the first two years before the interest rate jumped to a market rate. This increase could almost double the rate with a large jump in the monthly payment. Mortgage lenders offered what were called low-doc and no-doc loans—that is, loans made without credit checks or other traditional lending considerations and documents. These loans were cynically called liar loans, since the information on the credit applica-tion was rarely, if ever, verified. In an effort to keep them honest, the mortgage brokers were required to keep a small percentage of their loans on their books or to buy back any loans that quickly went into default. Despite this exposure, most brokers saw no reason to worry about repayment and creditworthiness, since conventional wisdom at the time held that home prices would continue rising into the foresee-able future, and those loans would be refinanced or paid off upon sale of the home before default.

Repackaging subprime mortgages into bonds became a huge money machine for the investment banks. In his book *The Big Short*, Michael Lewis explained how the mortgage companies and the investment banks earned billions of dollars in fees by recycling money between bond investors worldwide and American home buyers. The risk of default for the most part was transferred with those bonds. Bond buy-ers were lulled by triple A credit ratings for the bonds despite the sub-prime quality of the mortgages backing them. The poster child for this lending orgy according to Lewis was a California farmworker making $14,000 per year who received a home loan of over $700,000. As men-tioned above, the underpinning of this debt debacle was the belief that ever-rising home values would allow otherwise unqualified borrowers to either refinance the debt or sell the property at a profit before the two year teaser rates increased. Once the interest rates went up, the loans became unaffordable. Since the mortgage brokers and investment bankers had only a fractional interest in the loans and bonds after they were sold to investors or they had laid off the risk with credit default swaps, they did not believe they could suffer any loss. What they failed to appreciate was the fact that even a small fractional interest in hundreds of billions of dollars is still a large number.

The results of this played out when an unexpectedly large percentage of the loans started to go into default. The other part of this perfect storm was the rapid decline in home values. Mortgage debt exceeded the value of the collateral with the obvious result—billions of dollars in losses for the holders of the mortgage-backed bonds around the world. As the music started to slow down in 2007, several very large, publicly traded mortgage companies went out of business.

Signs that the party was truly over were the failures of two venerable Wall Street firms, Bear Stearns and Lehman Brothers, in 2008. The exposure of both Bear Stearns and Lehman to the subprime mortgage market played a significant role in their failures. Lehman's September 15, 2008 bankruptcy filing, considered one of the largest in history, foretold the credit crisis to come.

10

Mutual Funds

Pooled investing has been around for centuries. Many financial historians point to a Dutch investment trust (called a negotiatie) as the first such investment, which was established in 1774. Its stated purpose was to provide diversification to individual investors at a small cost. The organizer of the first trust, Adriaan van Ketwich, organized a second one in 1779 that remained in existence for 114 years. It was dissolved in 1893, the same year The Boston Personal Property Trust, one of the first American investment trusts, was formed.

The forebearer of the modern American mutual fund, the Massachusetts Investors' Trust, was established as an open-end fund in Boston in 1924. The Wellington Fund, launched in 1928, was the first mutual fund to invest specifically in stocks and bonds, a balanced fund. The value investor, Philip Carret, was one of the organizers of the Pioneer Fund in 1928. Pioneer is still in business today. The number of funds increased over time, but many were wiped out during the 1929 Wall Street crash. Investigations into these failures revealed a fair amount of chicanery and self-dealing on the part of the operators of the failed mutual funds. This led to the passage of The Investment Company Act of 1940, which placed numerous restrictions on the operations of US mutual funds and required certain disclosures to investors. The act was also written to reduce the conflicts of interest revealed in the investigations.

Over the years the popularity of mutual funds has waxed and waned. Mutual funds grew rapidly during the 1960s, but the number dropped precipitously after the bear market of 1969, with only 360 funds remaining in 1970. Later, two tax law changes gave the industry a big boost. The individual retirement account (IRA) and a form of retirement plan known by the tax section that authorized it, the 401(k), provided large platforms for the sale of mutual funds to millions of Americans saving for their golden years. Interest in mutual funds dropped again in 2003 with the revelation of widespread scandals in which a number of funds were alleged to have allowed their large hedge fund customers to engage in abusive trade-timing practices at the expense of their smaller customers.

Memories are short on Wall Street, and the mutual fund industry has recovered since 2003. It is reported that there were approximately fourteen thousand mutual funds, including money market funds, in existence in 2011. The funds offer every sort of investment strategy in stocks, corporate bonds, government debt, gold, oil, and any other investment asset you can think of. The irony is that year in and year out, a large number of the funds (some say as high as 80 percent of them) fail to meet or beat the annual performance of their respective market benchmarks.

POOLED INVESTMENT BASICS

There are four types of pooled investments, technically referred to as investment companies: open-end investment companies, closed-end investment companies, exchange-traded funds, and unit-investment trusts.

The most familiar type, the open-end, is what is commonly known as a mutual fund. The shares of the fund do not trade in the market;

however, investors can quickly and easily purchase and redeem their shares from the fund sponsor. The net asset value (NAV) of a fund and, hence, the value of its shares are based on the value of the investments in the fund. A fund's NAV is calculated and announced at the end of each trading day. NAV is the sum of any cash reserves and the closing prices of all of the securities held in the fund less liabilities, if any. That number is then divided by the number of shares the investors hold. This price then holds for fund-share purchases and redemptions until the end of the next trading day, when a new NAV is determined.

A closed-end fund is organized and traded basically as a stock. The fund is offered to investors in a form of initial public offering. The money is used to purchase stocks, bonds, or any other investment assets based on the strategy the fund is to follow. Unlike a mutual fund, this fund is closed to new money. The shares of a closed-end fund trade in the market just like a stock. The price of closed-end shares may be higher (a premium) or lower (a discount) than the actual NAV of the fund for any number of reasons, such as the basic rule of supply and demand, perceived prospects for future growth, decline of the fund's assets, and all the other reasons prices rise and fall in an active market.

An exchange-traded fund (ETF) is a hybrid security. Essentially an ETF is a mutual fund; however, it trades in the market just like a closed-end fund or a stock. ETFs do not have a NAV set daily. Rather, the value of an ETF fluctuates during the day, like a stock. Many ETFs contain pools of stocks that mirror a market index, like the S&P 500. In fact, the first ETF was an S&P 500 index fund, commonly referred to as a spider since its ticker symbol is SPDR. Some ETFs only invest in certain sectors of the market, such as car manufacturers, health care, emerging markets, and virtually any other area of the market you can name. As with stocks, an investor can short ETFs and buy them on margin. The management fees and transaction costs of operating an ETF index fund are generally lower than those of an index mutual fund.

A unit-investment trust (UIT) combines several features of the other three investment companies. Like a closed-end fund, the sponsor offers a fixed number of units in the trust to investors in a public offering. The offering proceeds are invested in securities that remain the same for the life of the UIT. There is little if any change in the portfolio over its lifetime. Unlike the other pooled investments, the UIT has a termination date, at which point the securities in the trust portfolio are sold, and the cash is distributed to the investors. Like a mutual fund, units may be purchased or sold. However, the units are traded on a secondary market maintained by the sponsor. The sponsor itself does not buy and sell units.

MUTUAL FUNDS—BEHIND THE CURTAIN

Investing in a mutual fund requires little more than money and some keystrokes on your computer or a phone call to your broker. Notwithstanding the simplicity of interaction, there is a lot going on behind the curtain—much like in *The Wizard of Oz*. Establishing and operating a typical mutual fund consists of a number of different functions.

The sponsor of the fund organizes the fund and provides the seed money to get it started. The sponsor, as the first shareholder, establishes an initial board of directors to manage the fund. Once people invest in the fund, they become the fund's shareholders and elect directors. Typically the sponsor is also the investment adviser, directing the fund's investments and managing the portfolio. This key function could, however, be handled by a different company.

Administrators perform the back-office operations. They provide the various things needed to run a fund, such as office space, clerical staff, internal accounting, and the filing of reports with the SEC and the Internal Revenue Service. Mutual fund investors buy and redeem their shares in the fund through an underwriter. The underwriter agrees with the mutual fund to buy and sell shares of the fund to the public. Transfer agents keep track of the accounts and calculate each investor's share of dividends and capital gains distributions. They also provide account statements, notices, and income tax information to the shareholders. The fund's portfolio of stocks, bonds, or other investment assets are usually held in the name of a custodian. An outside accounting firm audits the books and records of the fund and provides the required opinions concerning its financial status. In short, a fund has a lot of moving parts, and each party playing a role must be paid. Hence the fees and expenses charged the shareholders.

Mutual funds fall into two general categories: active and passive management. The portfolio of an actively managed fund is overseen by an investment adviser with the goal of beating a recognized market average, such as the S&P 500 Index. This is a difficult job, and a majority of funds fail to reach this goal in any given year. This gives rise to a good deal of debate as to the true benefits of actively managed mutual funds. On a worldwide basis, mutual funds of all kinds invest trillions (yes, that's with a *T*) of dollars annually. In recent years the number of funds in the United States has exceeded the number of individual stocks listed on the NYSE and the NASDAQ.

In effect mutual funds, collectively, *are* the market. Their combined trading of stocks creates a significant percentage of annual market volume and movement—in effect the market average. It is simple mathematics. If you deduct their expenses and fees, most mutual funds stand little or no chance of beating the market average their collective investing has created. In addition to the drag on annual returns from fees and expenses, mutual fund returns must also be reduced by the income taxes generated during the fund's tax year unless held in a tax-deferred retirement account, such as an IRA or a 401(k). Under the US federal tax code, mutual funds are pass-through entities. The shareholders, not the fund, pay the income taxes.

Mutual funds annually distribute all dividends received and capital gains generated in the portfolio to their shareholders. The shareholders can receive their shares of the distribution either in the form of checks or by reinvestment in shares of the fund. Most distributions are made in December of each year. If an investor buys shares in the mutual fund just before a distribution, the investor incurs a tax liability on the entire year's worth of income even though he or she may have held the shares for only a month or so. There have been loss years in which the mutual fund shareholders watched the value of their investments decline but still had to pay capital gains tax. When the dot-com bubble burst, many mutual funds that had invested early in high-tech stocks ended the year with losses. Despite the losses, the funds had sold quite a bit of the stock they had earlier purchased at much lower prices to meet redemptions, thus generating capital gains. The shareholders had to not only watch their investments lose money but also send checks to the IRS for gains that were of no economic benefit to them.

Much has been written about the apparent inability of a majority of actively managed funds to beat general market averages. In his 2003 book *Investment Philosophies,* Professor Aswath Damodaran of the New York University Stern School of Business cited three behavioral factors that might be seen to contribute to this shortfall in return: lack of investment consistency, herd behavior, and the practice of window dressing. A mutual fund's prospectus states its goals and the investment philosophy it will use to reach them. Unfortunately studies have revealed that investment advisers will pay only lip service to these stated objectives in times of market turmoil. Fund managers have been seen to repeatedly switch their investment styles in response to the latest market moves, up or down.

The second factor, herding, is a basic human trait. Human beings tend to act collectively, much like other species. With so many market professionals engaged in the same activity, it should be no surprise that institutional investors tend to buy and sell the same stocks at roughly the same time. This magnified action will tend to drive stocks up or down to a greater degree than might otherwise be expected. The third behavioral factor, window dressing, also reflects human nature. It is well documented that fund portfolios are subject to a noticeable amount of trading close to the dates on which the funds must report their results and reveal their shareholdings. The losers are sold, and the most recent market winners are purchased just prior to reporting results. The basis for this might be, in part, the cynical belief that the investing public will pay more attention to the reported portfolio holdings than the actual returns made during the period. Such activity is self-defeating, since it results in increased trading costs and a concomitant decline in returns.

JOHN C. BOGLE—THE GODFATHER OF MUTUAL FUNDS

John C. Bogle, the founder of The Vanguard Group, explained the popularity of mutual funds in his 1994 book *Bogle on Mutual Funds: New Perspectives for the Intelligent Investor*:

> While the wide selection of mutual fund offerings has provided much of the impetus for the industry's growth during the past two decades [he is speaking of the 1970s and 1980s], four time-honored principles of mutual fund investing are the core of the industry's success. These principles are (1) broad diversification, (2) professional management, (3) liquidity, and (4) convenience. They remain as valid today as they were when the first U.S. mutual fund was introduced.[1]

The Vanguard Group offer a wide variety of mutual funds (and the first index fund) to the public, and Bogle's book explains how to invest in them. He decried the habit of some investors of focusing only on past performance when looking for a mutual fund. He labeled it "a flawed and counterproductive way to select a mutual fund."[2] He recommended looking at a fund's structural characteristics as well as performance. He suggested every investor, when looking for a suitable mutual fund, check the following.

Three of the most obvious characteristics are the size of a fund, its age, and the tenure of the managers. Bogle suggested investing in funds in existence for at least five years with more than $50 million and less than $1 billion in assets. You should also look to see how long the portfolio managers have been running the fund. Assume that the past performance of a fund is due for a change if the investment managers who generated earlier returns are no longer in charge. Another characteristic to consider is the cost of owning shares in a fund. Are there sales charges when you buy and redemption charges when you sell? Bogle advised investors to search for no-load funds. Funds are required to publish their expense ratios, so an investor should compare them when deciding between funds. The lower the ratio, the more money remains for the shareholders.

Of primary importance is the fund's portfolio. The investor must learn a fund's cash position, since all funds have to keep some cash reserves. To Mr. Bogle it made no sense to pay advisory fees to someone just to hold cash. He recommended avoiding funds with cash positions of more than 5 percent of total assets. Portfolio concentration is another area to investigate. The investor should look at the top ten stock holdings of a fund and determine what percentage of the total portfolio these ten holdings represent. If the top ten stocks comprise more than 50 percent of the total holdings, Bogle felt there is a good possibility of the fund providing extraordinary performance. Unfortunately that performance can be either positive or negative. Also check to see if the fund is really a disguised sector fund, with a concentration in only one or two industries. Another important characteristic is the market capitalization of the stocks in the portfolio. Bogle pointed out that you will find an average market cap of $5 billion to $8 billion for the individual stocks found in a typical stock fund.

Since taxes and expenses must be considered, the investor should also confirm a fund's turnover rate. This reveals what percentage of a fund's assets are bought and sold in a one-year period. A high rate (some funds' rates exceed 100 percent) indicates potentially higher expenses, trading costs, and taxes to be borne by the fund holders. Check to see how often securities in a fund are purchased and sold in a year. A fund devoted to a long-term strategy should have a lower turnover rate than a fund focused on quick trading profits.

Keep in mind that successful investing for an individual investor is not the same as being a success on Wall Street. A professional money manager is a success on Wall Street when he or she is able to attract the most money from people who have accepted the idea that they cannot do their own investing. The more money an investment fund manager can attract, the more fees and charges that fund manager earns. Whether his or her investment strategy actually makes the most money for the investors is only important insofar as such success attracts yet more investor money, which translates into yet more fees. As I have said repeatedly in this book, the folks on Wall Street are entitled to earn a living; however, the individual investor can save those fees and charges if he or she takes the time and makes the effort to learn how to invest.

In short, investing in a mutual fund requires as much research and study as purchasing an individual stock. If an individual must work just as hard for either type of investment, is there an easier way? The answer is yes. Look for an index mutual fund, which was first offered to the public by Mr. Bogle.

INDEX FUNDS—IF YOU CAN'T BEAT THE MARKET, BUY IT

I assume older investors (I count myself as one of them) can remember the days before index funds, but younger investors might be surprised to learn that one of the most popular mutual funds today, the S&P 500 Index Fund, is not yet fifty years old. Professor Burton G. Malkiel, the famous proponent of the random walk theory, lamented the lack of a mutual fund focused on market averages as follows: "What we need is a no-load, minimum management-fee mutual fund that simply buys the hundreds of stocks making up the broad stock-market averages and does no trading from security to security in an attempt to catch the winners. Whenever below-average performance on the part of a mutual fund is noticed, fund salesmen are quick to point out 'You can't buy the averages.' It's time the public could."[3]

He also wrote an article in the May 29, 2013 *Wall Street Journal* titled "You're Paying Too Much for Investment Help." In the article he analyzed the costs and expenses charged by actively managed mutual funds and concluded that investors looking for a better return should focus on index funds instead. He advised investors that while they have no control over the market, they can control their cost to invest in it.

An index fund essentially holds a portfolio of stocks that mirrors an index such as the S&P 500, the thirty stocks in the Dow Jones Average, or some other index of market assets, such as the Wilshire 5,000 Total Stock Market Index. Index funds were initially available only to institutional investors in the early 1970s. John Bogle's company, Vanguard, was the first to offer the index fund to individual investors, the Vanguard S&P 500 Index Fund. Once the index of stocks has been duplicated, trading is minimal, since the fund advisers need only to rebalance the fund depending on what happens to the stocks comprising the index. This provides the individual investor with the opportunity to buy a particular market with a low expense ratio.

Given this background, an individual could rightfully ask whether it matters which particular index fund he or she purchases if they track the same index. Won't two S&P 500 Index funds produce the same results? Sadly, the answer is "not necessarily."

Although the costs and expenses of an index fund are lower than actively managed funds, they still exist. The operation of an index fund involves almost all of the same functions as an active fund except for portfolio management. A larger fund can spread those costs over more investors. Another drag on returns is the efficiency with which a fund can buy and sell stocks, the execution/trading costs it incurs. Some smaller funds find it too expensive to actually buy all of the stocks in an index. They try to duplicate the index by the process of sampling. Sampling means that the fund designs a stock portfolio with the same characteristics as the total index. Keep in mind that a sample will not provide the same return as the total index. Hopefully the costs and expenses saved by sampling are passed along to the fund's shareholders to make up for the lower return they might receive.

To see how closely the return of an index fund tracks the return of the actual index, the investor could look at the R-squared rating of the fund. R-squared is a mathematical measure of the difference in returns. If the fund's return is identical to that of the index, the R-squared is 100 percent. Virtually all funds fall short due to their costs of operation and execution. Professor Damodaran, in his book *Investment Philosophies*, suggested that investors check Morningstar rankings of index funds to find out what their R-squared percentages are. He advised investors to find funds with the lowest expenses and the highest R-squareds.

Investment Management is a book with chapters written by investment professionals and edited by Peter L. Bernstein and Professor Damodaran. The advantages of index funds are described in the book as follows:

First, no information costs or analyst expenses are associated with running these funds, and transaction costs associated with trading are low. Most index funds have turnover ratios of less than 5 percent, indicating that the total dollar volume of trading was less than 5 percent of the market values of the funds. Transaction costs for these funds are 0.20 percent to 0.50 percent, or less than one-third the costs of most actively managed funds. Second, the index funds' reticence to trade reduces the tax liabilities that they create for investors. In a typical actively managed fund, the high turnover ratios create capital gains and tax liabilities even for those investors who buy and hold these funds.[4]

Index funds are the answer for individuals who do not have the time or the inclination to invest in individual stocks, but want a low cost way to invest their money in equities.

11

Retirement Investing

RETIREMENT—YOUR SECOND FIRST JOB

Congratulations! You made it to retirement. As the title of this section points out, you now have a new job. During your working career, the majority of your retirement savings have, in all likelihood, been managed by a pension administrator or a 401(k) plan provider. In other words, while you were busy with your career, someone else was making most of the investment decisions for your retirement portfolio. They provided your investment choices. Like many others, you will probably choose to receive a lump sum transfer of those 401(k) proceeds into an individual retirement account (IRA) after you have wrapped up your last days of work.

You are now sitting at the kitchen table on that first morning of your golden years, wondering where all the time went. At some point you will ponder the question of whether you will outlive your savings. Your new job, what I call your second first job, is to make sure the money is there for you through your remaining years (hopefully decades).

When Social Security was created in 1935, the retirement age (when benefits could first be received) was set at sixty-five. There were approximately 7.8 million people that age at the time, but average life expectancy then for men was fifty-eight and sixty-two for women. Today, a sixty-five-year-old enjoying reasonably good health can expect to live at least an additional twenty years. A single man's money has to last that long. Since women have longer life expectancies, a couple must make the expectancy calculation based on the longevity prospects for the wife.

A typical retiree will have three sources of income: Social Security, proceeds from an employer's retirement benefit program [pension or 401(k) plan], and personal retirement savings (an IRA).

As I mentioned earlier, there are three certainties in this life: death, taxes, and inflation. Of the three, inflation is a retiree's worst financial enemy. The annual inflation rate is low these days, but anyone sixty-five or older will remember when annual inflation rates were double digits. There is no reason to believe that this could not happen again in the next twenty or so years. Even low inflation rates, over time, will significantly erode the purchasing power of a retiree's income.

You may remember my earlier discussion of the old rule of thumb regarding asset allocation, which calls for a person's portfolio to consist of a percentage of debt securities equal to his or her age with the balance invested in equities. At the age of sixty-five, you should have 35 percent of your retirement funds in equities under the rule. As with all rules of thumb, the rule of age allocation cannot be followed blindly. Setting your allocation percentages is not a "one and done" decision. You should expect to change your allocation over time, as circumstances dictate. There are a couple of other factors to keep in mind.

SOCIAL SECURITY AND ASSET ALLOCATION

When considering their portfolio's division between equity and debt, many retirees look at their retirement savings as the only assets that must be considered in arriving at their debt and equity percentages. Many seniors do not think of their monthly Social Security checks as retirement assets, but they most certainly are. I believe your Social Security benefit should play a part in formulating your portfolio allocation.

Miles Goodwin

AARP, formerly the American Association of Retired Persons, recently reported that the average 401(k) balance for individuals in the fifty-five-plus age category had reached $255,000. Let's assume, for the sake of discussion, that by the age of sixty-five the combined 401(k) and IRA balances of a retiree have reached $400,000. This sum constitutes his or her entire retirement savings. How to invest that money? Following the traditional age-based allocation rule, 65 percent of the portfolio ($260,000) would be invested in debt securities, such as a savings account, certificate of deposit, US Treasuries, state or municipal obligations, and corporate bonds. The balance, $140,000, would go into publicly traded stocks or mutual funds—that is, equity securities.

However, if you consider your Social Security check as a monthly interest payment you receive on a government debt obligation that you **own**, those dollar allocations change. The first step is to find the interest rate on a one-year US Treasury obligation. This information is available every day in *The Wall Street Journal*. Assume you receive a monthly benefit of $1,000 from Social Security—$12,000 per year. Assume further that the current interest rate on a one-year Treasury is 3 percent per annum. Your hypothetical treasury obligation generating a 3 percent return of $12,000 would have an imaginary or notional principal value of $400,000 ($400,000 x 3 percent = $12,000). In effect you may now consider that you have an $800,000 retirement portfolio consisting of $400,000 in a hypothetical one-year 3 percent Treasury obligation and your actual $400,000 in cash. Under the age-based allocation, a total portfolio of $800,000 would then be allocated between $520,000 of debt securities (65 percent) and $280,000 of equity securities (35 percent) for a sixty-five-year-old. Given the $400,000 notional value of your Social Security investment, your cash could then be divided into $120,000 of actual interest-bearing securities and $280,000 of stocks or mutual funds. Under this scenario your retirement fund, on a cash basis, could contain twice the equity securities it would if you did not include the Social Security debt obligation in your allocation decision.

Once a year, maybe each January, you should recheck the going interest rate for one-year Treasuries. You then recalculate the present value of your Social Security investment based on your monthly checks (which are increased by an annual cost-of-living adjustment) and reallocate between debt and equity. As stated earlier, asset allocation is not a one-time decision. You should revisit it at least annually. The age-based reallocation need not be precise year by year. During your sixties you might just allocate 65 percent debt for the entire decade. As you age, the debt percentage of the portfolio goes up accordingly. If interest rates on government obligations are very low, you may want to look at the rates on Treasuries of a longer duration. Simply assuming a 3 percent rate of interest in these days of very low rates may be a conservative way to calculate your notional Social Security obligation.

Financial advisers have touted the age-based allocation for many years; however, with the extended longevity expected for today's retirees, it may be necessary to consider an allocation that results in a larger portion of equity in your portfolio than called for under the basic age formula. The addition of the hypothetical Social Security investment to the debt side of a portfolio helps to accomplish this. Equities have proven to be better than debt securities for minimizing the effects of inflation on a retiree's portfolio and lifestyle.

A retiree must also take the present state of the market into account in establishing his or her allocation between debt and equity securities. Is the market rising, declining, or moving sideways? Some consideration of the market is necessary when deciding how to split your portfolio. As the market or the value of your equities changes, you may need to rebalance your asset allocation.

Of more importance than the state of the market is your state of mind. I have repeatedly advised you to honestly determine your risk tolerance. Warren Buffett said if you could not tolerate a decline of 50 percent in your equity portfolio's value without selling out your position, you should probably not invest in individual stocks. Over your remaining years, the market will rise and fall several times, carrying a portfolio of common stocks with it. If a drop of 50 percent in value will likely lead you to panic selling, your equity allocation should be smaller than that of an investor who is psychologically able to ride out the market storm. It is said that someone once told J. P. Morgan that frequent changes in the value of his portfolio caused him to lose sleep. He asked what he should do about it. Morgan's famous reply was, "Sell down until you can sleep." Although anecdotal, the advice may be a good way to decide how much you keep in equities. Retirement is supposed to be enjoyable, not nerve wracking. As mentioned earlier, you can take the Risk Tolerance Quiz created by Professors Grable and Lytton in the Appendix to get an idea of your ability to handle market turbulence and investment risk.

DO YOU REALLY HAVE A NUMBER?

The most frequent question asked by the soon-to-be retired individual focuses on how large a portfolio he or she needs. Remember the TV investment ads with the tagline "What's your number?" Fred Schwed, in his book *Where Are the Customers' Yachts? or A Good Hard Look At Wall Street* pointed out an interesting difference between American and British investors:

> The British, as a race, have been engaged with the problems of capital investment for a longer period than we have, and accordingly have reached a greater maturity regarding it. Have you noticed that when you ask a Britisher about a man's wealth you get an answer quite different from that an American gives you? The American says, "I wouldn't be surprised if he's worth

close to a million dollars." The Englishman says, "I fancy he has five thousand pounds a year." The Englishman's habitual way of speaking and thinking about wealth is of course much closer to the nub of the matter. A man's true wealth is his income, not his bank balance.[1]

You have been saving, investing, and growing your retirement portfolio during your working career. As a retiree you should now think like the British and focus on replacing your salary. The question is how to make your retirement savings last for the foreseeable future.

In the 1990s William Bengen, a certified financial planner, studied this issue. He made three assumptions: the portfolio was in an IRA or other tax-deferred account, the retiree did not intend to leave any inheritance, and the savings had to last for thirty years. Based on those premises, he calculated that a retiree would not outlive his or her savings if withdrawals were limited to 4 percent of the account valued annually.

As with all other financial research and rules, not everyone agrees with Bengen's 4 percent rule. Some look to the condition of the market at the time of retirement as a factor. If the market is down or in danger of decline in the near future when you leave the workforce, 4 percent may be too much to take out at the beginning of your retirement. If the market is rising and a retiree has a high-risk tolerance (severe stock market fluctuations do not bother the individual), the rate might be set higher than 4 percent. Like asset allocation rules, deciding on a rate of withdrawal is not a one-time decision. You should revisit both asset allocation and withdrawal rates annually. You might consider the 4 percent rule as a starting point for your first year of retirement.

Let's return to your $800,000 combined hypothetical and cash portfolio. Using the 4 percent rule, this means you can withdraw 4 percent of your $800,000 portfolio ($32,000) annually with the goal of making your assets last thirty more years. You are receiving $12,000, which is 3 percent of the $400,000 hypothetical value of your Social Security account. In order to maintain an average annual withdrawal rate of 4 percent, this means you might withdraw up to 5 percent of your $400,000 from the combined equities and debt portfolio in your cash IRA. Your retirement income of $32,000 would consist of the Social Security payments of $12,000 plus $20,000 (5 percent of $400,000) from your IRA. If you are conservative and want to remain true to the 4 percent rule, you would withdraw only $16,000 of your cash portfolio (4 percent of $400,000) for a total income of $28,000. Obviously you would want to preserve your princial by first withdrawing the interest and dividends generated in your IRA before selling any assets. If that is not enough, the balance would have to come from principal.

The hope is that your equity holdings will appreciate at a rate greater than your withdrawal rate, so your portfolio either remains the same or increases. Another way to handle this might be to take out only the income generated by your portfolio. In all probability you would then be taking out less than 4 percent from the total portfolio. Conversely you could increase your withdrawal rate to maintain your standard of living. Keep in mind that with a higher withdrawal rate, your savings may not last as long as needed. You might allocate more assets to equities for a potentially higher yearly return, but this would expose your portfolio to a greater degree of market risk. To sustain a desired lifestyle, you might make a greater equity allocation, a higher withdrawal rate, or both. You have to decide if you can comfortably take on greater market risk. Again, what is your risk tolerance?

Your risk tolerance, whether you have measured it or not, is the basis of your investing style. Your personal risk tolerance level will define your ability to withstand the basic investing emotions: fear and greed. These inner pressures affect most investors as their portfolios move up or down with the market. As we have learned, Justin Mamis, the famous technical investor and author, felt that your view of risk is formed, in part, in your childhood, and your risk tolerance informs your method of making investment decisions. In his 1991 book *The Nature of Risk, Stock Market Survival and the Meaning of Life*, he discussed this phenomenon as follows:

Americans are often described as basically optimistic, when in reality it is that they are perpetually hopeful. The market seems to represent hope itself. And yet, among professionals, even those who function on the stock exchange floor, a frequently heard stock market expression is, "No one ever said it was going to be easy." It never can be easy because the rule of the market is that you have to act before you know enough. Because it is a process there is no one moment or single point, at which one can make an obvious "sure" decision.

Thus it is not just information that becomes the key to taking a market risk; it is also necessary to understand such information in terms of our relationship to that knowledge. "What do we know?" "How do we know it?" and "What is our reaction to that information?"—as well as "What do we need/wish/want to know?"—are all questions that affect the decisions we make every day. When a decision is required, the way we take information in, and how we use it, affects that decision. Our self's style goes back deep into childhood. The manner in which we let information in, our ability to understand it, to deal with it, and perhaps even distort it, all start with who we are, as developed from the moment of beginning, on our hands and knees, to explore the world.

Thus the risk we are about to take via our next decision is not a simple choice of "do it or not" or "yes or no." Before deciding, we need to know why what we know is never enough, a question that, in turn, leads to what kind of information do we believe or trust? And is it us or the market? But we must remember that there are times when the market, or life itself, is incoherent, unclear, and/or conflicting: times when it isn't us, it's it. The risk can never be cured by knowing enough.[2]

As an investor (retired or not), you cannot control what you do not recognize. Understand your risk tolerance, and adjust your investing accordingly.

11

Final Thoughts

ENOUGH IS ENOUGH

As we have seen, an individual must set a goal as the first step in any investment plan. Why are you investing? What is the purpose for the money you hope to make with the investment? Saving for a rainy day or for a child's college tuition each requires a different investment strategy. The strategy for both of them will differ from the strategy for investing a retirement portfolio. The Cat in Lewis Carroll's classic *Alice's Adventures in Wonderland* gave Alice the following answer to her request for directions:

> "Would you tell me, please, which way I ought to go from here?"
> "That depends a good deal on where you want to go to," said the Cat.[1]

Ben Graham advised individuals that they should not invest to beat the market. Rather, the investor should focus on achieving his or her specific investment goal. Al Frank, author of *Al Frank's New Prudent Speculator*, cited the fourth-century book of Chinese philosophy, *Tao Te Ching*. The pertinent verse of the *Tao* states, "Going to extremes is never best...The way to success is this: having achieved your goal, be satisfied not to go further. For this is the way Nature operates."[2]

In his book *Where Are the Customers' Yachts?*, Fred Schwed, Jr. asked the following questions:

> If a man makes thirty million dollars, and then loses the entire thirty million and some more to boot, would you say that such a man is quite bright in the head? I should like to carry this inquiry into intelligence a little further and ask a second question: what do you think of the mentality of a man who goes down to Wall Street with very little and wins, by speculation, thirty millions, none of which he has as yet lost? My own considered opinion is that he too is pretty loony. In order to make his second unimportant million he had to risk his first precious million. Obviously he did so, and did it time and again. That he happens to have been successful each time does not really change the picture. What **could** he have been thinking of each time he took all those risks? The very contemplation of it makes my bourgeois soul shudder.[3] [Author's emphasis in **bold**.]

Some folks still believe the mantra from the 1990s that "More is better." I would suggest more is just more and enough is enough.

LAST WORDS

It seems appropriate to end with final thoughts from several of the authors we have met.

Ben Graham ended *The Intelligent Investor* with these parting words: "We are not going to end with J. J. Raskob's slogan that we made fun of at the beginning: 'Everybody can be rich.' But interesting possibilities abound on the financial scene, and the intelligent and enterprising investor should be able to find both enjoyment and profit in this three-ring circus. Excitement is guaranteed."[4]

Burton Malkiel concluded with an analogy for investing in *A Random Walk Down Wall Street*: "Investing is a bit like lovemaking. Ultimately, it is really an art requiring a certain talent and the presence of a mysterious force called luck. Indeed, luck may be 99 percent responsible for the success of the very few people who have beaten the averages...The game of investing is like lovemaking in another important respect, too. It's much too much fun to give up."[5]

Peter Lynch listed his twenty golden rules for investing at the conclusion of *Beating the Street*, and the following is one of them: "Owning stocks is like having children—don't get involved with more than you can handle. The part-time stockpicker probably has time to follow 8–12 companies, and to buy and sell shares as conditions warrant. There don't have to be more than 5 companies in the portfolio at any one time."[6]

Jesse Livermore may have summed it up best in *How to Trade in Stocks*: "There is nothing new on Wall Street or in stock speculation. What has happened in the past will happen again, and again, and again. This is because human nature does not change, and it is human emotion, solidly built into human nature, that always gets in the way of human intelligence. Of this I am sure."[7]

Thank you for reading.

AFTERWORD

I have tried my level best to remain neutral and simply explain the various forms of investing without recommendation on my part. I admit to making some observations, which have tended more toward "don't" than "do." But every writer usually ends with some advice, so here goes.

If, after finishing this book, you have concluded that "The Game," as Adam Smith called it, is not for you, but you realize your need to invest in any event, I recommend you return to the chapter on mutual funds and carefully reread Professor Burton Malkiel's advice regarding index funds.

For those of you who have discovered within yourselves the propensity for investing identified by Lord Keynes, your reading task has just begun. Look at the list of texts in the beginning of this book; find the book and strategy that appeals to you, and dive in. With a slight change to Sherlock Holmes's exhortation to Watson in one of their cases, I would say, "Come, Watson, come! The Game is afoot."[1]

APPENDIX

RISK TOLERANCE QUIZ¹ WITH SCORING GRID

Want to improve your personal finances? Start by taking this quiz to get an idea of your investment risk tolerance – one of the fundamental issues to consider when planning your investment strategy, either alone or in consultation with a financial services professional. The *Investment Risk Tolerance Quiz* is also available online at http://njaes.rutgers.edu/money/riskquiz/.

Choose the response that best describes you – there are no "right" or "wrong" answers. Just have fun!

When you're done, click on the "View Results" button to see how you're doing.

Note: By taking this quiz you will be contributing to a study on measuring financial risk tolerance. Your results will be recorded anonymously. We are not collecting any identifying information.

1.   In general, how would your best friend describe you as a risk taker?

    a.   A real gambler

    b.   Willing to take risks after completing adequate research

c.   Cautious

d.   A real risk avoider

2.   You are on a TV game show and can choose one of the following. Which would you take?

a. $1,000 in cash

b.   A 50% chance at winning $5,000

c.   A 25% chance at winning $10,000

d.   A 5% chance at winning $100,000

3.   You have just finished saving for a "once-in-a-lifetime" vacation. Three weeks before you plan to leave, you lose your job. You would:

a.   Cancel the vacation

b.   Take a much more modest vacation

c.   Go as scheduled, reasoning that you need the time to prepare for a job search

d.   Extend your vacation, because this might be your last chance to go first-class

4.   If you unexpectedly received $20,000 to *invest*, what would you do?

a.   Deposit it in a bank account, money market account, or an insured CD

b.   Invest it in safe high quality bonds or bond mutual funds

c.   Invest it in stocks or stock mutual funds

5.   In terms of experience, how comfortable are you investing in stocks or stock mutual funds?

a.   Not at all comfortable

b.   Somewhat comfortable

c.   Very comfortable

6.   When you think of the word "risk" which of the following words comes to mind first?

a.   Loss

b.   Uncertainty

c.   Opportunity

d.   Thrill

7.   Some experts are predicting prices of assets such as gold, jewels, collectibles, and real estate (hard assets) to increase in value; bond prices may fall, however, experts tend to agree that government bonds are relatively safe. Most of your investment assets are now in high interest government bonds. What would you do?

a.   Hold the bonds

b.   Sell the bonds, put half the proceeds into money market accounts, and the other half into hard assets

c.   Sell the bonds and put the total proceeds into hard assets

d.   Sell the bonds, put all the money into hard assets, and borrow additional money to buy more

8.   Given the best and worst case returns of the four investment choices below, which would you prefer?

a. $200 gain best case; $0 gain/loss worst case

b. $800 gain best case; $200 loss worst case

c. $2,600 gain best case; $800 loss worst case

d. $4,800 gain best case; $2,400 loss worst case

9. In addition to whatever you own, you have been given $1,000. You are now asked to choose between:
    a. A sure gain of $500
    b. A 50% chance to gain $1,000 and a 50% chance to gain nothing

10. In addition to whatever you own, you have been given $2,000. You are now asked to choose between:
    a. A sure loss of $500
    b. A 50% chance to lose $1,000 and a 50% chance to lose nothing

11. Suppose a relative left you an inheritance of $100,000, stipulating in the will that you invest **ALL** the money in **ONE** of the following choices. Which one would you select?
    a. A savings account or money market mutual fund
    b. A mutual fund that owns stocks and bonds
    c. A portfolio of 15 common stocks
    d. Commodities like gold, silver, and oil

12. If you had to invest $20,000, which of the following investment choices would you find most appealing?
    a. 60% in low-risk investments 30% in medium-risk investments 10% in high-risk investments
    b. 30% in low-risk investments 40% in medium-risk investments 30% in high-risk investments
    c. 10% in low-risk investments 40% in medium-risk investments 50% in high-risk investments

13. Your trusted friend and neighbor, an experienced geologist, is putting together a group of investors to fund an exploratory

gold mining venture. The venture could pay back 50 to 100 times the investment if successful. If the mine is a bust, the entire investment is worthless. Your friend estimates the chance of success is only 20%. If you had the money, how much would you invest?

a.   Nothing

b.   One month's salary

c.   Three month's salary

d.   Six month's salary

[1] Risk Tolerance Quiz Source: Grable, J. E., & Lytton, R. H. (1999). Financial risk tolerance revisited: The development of a risk assessment instrument. *Financial Services Review*, 8, 163-181.

RISK TOLERANCE QUIZ SCORING GRID

The scoring for the risk tolerance quiz questions is as follows:

1.   a=4; b=3; c=2; d=1

2.   a=1; b=2; c=3; d=4

3.   a=1; b=2; c=3; d=4

4.   a=1; b=2; c=3

5.   a=1; b=2; c=3

6.   a=1; b=2; c=3; d=4

7.   a=1; b=2; c=3; d=4

8.   a=1; b=2; c=3; d=4

9.   a=1; b=3

10.   a=1; b=3

11.   a=1; b=2; c=3; d=4

12.   a=1; b=2; c=3

13.   a=1; b=2; c=3; d=4

In general, the score that you receive on the *Investment Risk Tolerance Quiz* can be interpreted as follows:

18 or below = Low risk tolerance (i.e., conservative investor)

19 to 22 = Below-average risk tolerance

23 to 28 = Average/moderate risk tolerance

29 to 32 = Above-average risk tolerance

33 and above = High risk tolerance (i.e., aggressive investor)

End Notes

OPENING QUOTATION

1. Quotation from *Shibumi* by Trevanian, copyright © 1979 by Trevanian. Used by permission of Crown Books, an imprint of the Crown Publishing Group, a division of Penguin Random House LLC. All rights reserved. Any third party use of this material outside of this publication is prohibited. Interested parties must apply directly to Penguin Random House LLC for permission.

CHAPTER TWO: MARKETS

1. Benjamin Graham, *The Intelligent Investor—Revised Edition* (New York, NY: HarperCollins Publishers, Inc., 1973).

2. Adam Smith, *The Money Game* (New York, NY: Random House, Inc. 1967, 1968).

3. Charles McKay, *Extraordinary Popular Delusions and the Madness of Crowds* (New York, NY: John Wiley & Sons, Inc. 1841).

4. Gustave Le Bon, *The Crowd, A Study of the Popular Mind* (Mineola, NY: Dover Publications, Inc. 1895).

5. Ibid.

6. Justin Mamis, *The Nature of Risk, Stock Market Survival and the Meaning of Life* (Flint Hill, VA: Fraser Publishing Company, 1991).

7. Justin Mamis, *When to Sell—Inside Strategies for Stock-Market Profits* (Flint Hill, VA: Fraser Publishing Company, 1994).

8. Smith, *The Money Game.*

9. Norman G. Fosback, *Stock Market Logic, A Sophisticated Approach to Profits on Wall Street* (Deerfield Beach, FL: The Institute for Econometric Research, 1976, 1993).

10. Stephen J. Gould, *Full House, The Spread of Excellence from Plato to Darwin* (New York, NY: Random House, Inc., 1996).

11. Quotation from Louis Bachelier's 1900 doctoral thesis *The Theory of Speculation* is contained in *Capital Ideas / The Improbable Origins of Modern Wall Street* by Peter L. Bernstein.

12. Ibid.

13. Peter L. Bernstein, *Capital Ideas / The Improbable Origins of Modern Wall Street* (New York, NY: John Wiley & Sons, Inc., 1992).

14. Burton G. Malkiel, *A Random Walk Down Wall Street* (New York, NY: W. W. Norton & Company, Inc., 1973, 1981, 1985, 1990, 1999, 2003, 2007, 2011, 2012).

15. Fred Schwed, Jr., *Where Are the Customers' Yachts? Or A Good Hard Look at Wall Street* (New York, NY: John Wiley & Sons, Inc., 1940).

16. Mamis, *The Nature of Risk.*

CHAPTER THREE: INVESTORS

1. Justin Mamis, *The Nature of Risk, Stock Market Survival and the Meaning of Life* (Flint Hill, VA: Fraser Publishing Company, 1991).

2. Ibid.

3. Aswath Damodaran, *Investment Philosophies*, (New York, NY: John Wiley & Sons, Inc., 2003).

4. Philip L. Carret, *The Art of Speculation* (Flint Hill, VA: Fraser Publishing Company, 1930).

5. Benjamin Graham, *The Intelligent Investor—Revised Edition* (New York, NY: HarperCollins Publishers, Inc., 1973).

6. Al Frank, *Al Frank's New Prudent Speculator* (New York, NY: McGraw Hill, 1996).

7. Ibid.

8. Adam Smith, *The Money Game* (New York, NY: Random House, Inc. 1967, 1968).

9. Mamis, *The Nature of Risk*.

10. Smith, *The Money Game*.

11. Ibid.

12. Robert J. Shiller, *Irrational Exuberance* (Princeton, NJ: Princeton University Press, 2000).

13. Peter Lynch and John Rothchild, *One Up on Wall Street* (New York, NY: Simon & Schuster, Inc., 1989).

14. Fred Schwed, Jr., *Where Are the Customers'Yachts? Or A Good Hard Look at Wall Street* (New York, NY: John Wiley & Sons, Inc., 1940).

15. John Rothchild, *A Fool and His Money, The Odyssey of an Average Investor* (New York, NY: John Wiley & Sons, Inc., 1988, 1997).

16. Burton G. Malkiel, *A Random Walk Down Wall Street* (New York, NY: W. W. Norton & Company, Inc., 1973, 1981, 1985, 1990, 1999, 2003, 2007, 2011, 2012).

17. Justin Mamis, *When to Sell—Inside Strategies for Stock-Market Profits* (Flint Hill, VA: Fraser Publishing Company, 1994).

18. G. M. Loeb, *The Battle for Investment Survival* (Blacksburg, VA: Wilder Publications, Inc., 2010).

19. Smith, *The Money Game.*

20. Shiller, *Irrational Exuberance.*

21. Smith, *The Money Game.*

CHAPTER FOUR: INVESTMENT STRATEGIES: FUNDAMENTAL ANALYSIS

1. Philip L. Carret, *The Art of Speculation* (Flint Hill, VA: Fraser Publishing Company, 1930).

2. Carret, *The Art of Speculation* [all precepts in bold].

3. Warren E. Buffett, *Warren Buffett's Letters to Berkshire Shareholders* (Omaha, NE: Berkshire Hathaway, Inc., 1985).

4. Philip A. Fisher, *Common Stocks and Uncommon Profits* (New York, NY: John Wiley & Sons, Inc., 1996, 2003).

5. Humphrey B. Neill, *The Art of Contrary Opinion* (Caldwell, Idaho: Caxton Press, 1954, 1956, 1960, 1963).

6. Ibid.

7. David Dreman, *The New Contrarian Investment Strategy* (New York, NY: Random House, Inc., 1982).

8. Ibid.

9. Burton G. Malkiel, *A Random Walk Down Wall Street* (New York, NY: W. W. Norton & Company, Inc., 1973, 1981, 1985, 1990, 1999, 2003, 2007, 2011, 2012).

10. Ibid.

CHAPTER FIVE: INVESTMENT STRATEGIES: TECHNICAL ANALYSIS

1. Robert D. Edwards and John Magee, *Technical Analysis of Stock Trends* (New York, NY: AMACOM, 1948).

2. Norman G. Fosback, *Stock Market Logic, A Sophisticated Approach to Profits on Wall Street* (Deerfield Beach, FL: The Institute for Econometric Research, 1976, 1993).

3. Justin Mamis, *The Nature of Risk, Stock Market Survival and the Meaning of Life* (Flint Hill, VA: Fraser Publishing Company, 1991).

4. Humphrey B. Neill, *Tape Reading & Market Tactics* (Miami, FL: BN Publishing, 1931).

5. Fosback, *Stock Market Logic*.

6. Mamis, *The Nature of Risk*.

7. Justin Mamis, *When to Sell—Inside Strategies for Stock-Market Profits* (Flint Hill, VA: Fraser Publishing Company, 1994).

8. Neill, *Tape Reading & Market Tactics*.

9. John Maynard Keynes, *The General Theory of Employment, Interest and Money* (Amherst, NY: Prometheus Books, 1936).

10. Ibid.

11. Burton G. Malkiel, *A Random Walk Down Wall Street* (New York, NY: W. W. Norton & Company, Inc., 1973, 1981, 1985, 1990, 1999, 2003, 2007, 2011, 2012).

12. Ibid.

CHAPTER SIX: ADDITIONAL STRATEGIES
AND CONCLUSIONS

1. Burton G. Malkiel, *A Random Walk Down Wall Street* (New York, NY: W. W. Norton & Company, Inc., 1973, 1981, 1985, 1990, 1999, 2003, 2007, 2011, 2012).

2. Mark Twain, *The Tragedy of Pudd'nhead Wilson* (Hartford, CT: American Publishing Company, 1894).

3. Norman G. Fosback, *Stock Market Logic, A Sophisticated Approach to Profits on Wall Street* (Deerfield Beach, FL: The Institute for Econometric Research, 1976, 1993).

4. Mark Twain, *Following the Equator, A Journey Around the World* (Hartford CT: American Publishing Company, 1897).

5. Edwin Lefevre, *Reminiscences of a Stock Operator* (New York, NY: John Wiley & Sons, Inc., 1923).

6. Ibid.

7. Ibid.

8. Ibid.

9. Ibid.

10. John Kenneth Galbraith, *The Great Crash 1929* (Boston, MA: Houghton Mifflin Harcourt Publishing Company, 1954, 1955, 1961, 1972, 1979, 1988, 1997).

11. Humphrey B. Neill, *Tape Reading & Market Tactics* (Miami, FL: BN Publishing, 1931).

12. Jesse L. Livermore and Richard Smitten, *How to Trade in Stocks* (New York, NY: McGraw Hill, 1940).

13. Peter Lynch and John Rothchild, *Beating the Street* (New York, NY: Simon & Schuster, Inc., 1993).

14. Schwed, W*here Are the Customers' Yachts?*

15. Ibid.

CHAPTER SEVEN: SELLING

1. Jesse L. Livermore and Richard Smitten, *How to Trade in Stocks* (New York, NY: McGraw Hill, 1940).

2. Edwin Lefevre, *Reminiscences of a Stock Operator* (New York, NY: John Wiley & Sons, Inc., 1923).

CHAPTER EIGHT: THE COMPUTER—TIME
BOMB OR INVESTMENT TOOL

1. Adam Smith, *Paper Money* (New York, NY: Summit Books, 1981).

2. Peter L. Bernstein, *Capital Ideas/The Improbable Origins of Modern Wall Street* (New York, NY: John Wiley & Sons, Inc., 1992).

3. Nassim N. Taleb, *Fooled by Randomness—The Hidden Role of Chance in Life and the Markets* (New York, NY: Random House, Inc., 2004).

4. The Brady Commission, *Report of the Presidential Task Force on Market Mechanisms* (Jan. 1988).

5. Robert J. Shiller, *Irrational Exuberance* (Princeton, NJ: Princeton University Press, 2000).

6. Roger Lowenstein, *The Rise and Fall of Long-Term Capital Management, When Genius Failed* (New York, NY: Random House, Inc., 2000).

CHAPTER NINE: DEBT SECURITIES

1. William Shakespeare, *Hamlet*. Act 1, scene 3, 75–77. 1599–1602.

2. Benjamin Franklin, *Poor Richard's Almanack* (Philadelphia PA: B. Franklin, 1758).

3. "The Gambler" written by Don Schlitz and sung by Kenny Rogers, 1978.

4. Adam Smith, *Paper Money* (New York, NY: Summit Books, 1981).

CHAPTER TEN: MUTUAL FUNDS

1. John C. Bogle, *Bogle on Mutual Funds New Perspectives for the Intelligent Investor* (Burr Ridge, Il: Irwin Professional Publishing, 1994).

2. Ibid.

3. Burton G. Malkiel, *A Random Walk Down Wall Street* (New York, NY: W. W. Norton & Company, Inc., 1973, 1981, 1985, 1990, 1999, 2003, 2007, 2011, 2012).

4. Peter L. Bernstein and Aswath Damodaran, eds., *Investment Management* (New York, NY: John Wiley & Sons, Inc., 1998).

CHAPTER ELEVEN: RETIREMENT INVESTING

1. Fred Schwed, Jr., *Where Are the Customers' Yachts? Or A Good Hard Look at Wall Street* (New York, NY: John Wiley & Sons, Inc., 1940).

2. Justin Mamis, *The Nature of Risk, Stock Market Survival and the Meaning of Life* (Flint Hill, VA: Fraser Publishing Company, 1991).

CHAPTER TWELVE: FINAL THOUGHTS

1. Lewis Carroll. *Alice's Adventures in Wonderland* (London: Clarendon Press for Macmillan, 1865).

2. Lao Tzu, *Tao Te Ching* (sixth century BC).

3. Fred Schwed, Jr., *Where Are the Customers' Yachts? Or A Good Hard Look at Wall Street* (New York, NY: John Wiley & Sons, Inc., 1940).

4. Benjamin Graham, *The Intelligent Investor—Revised Edition* (New York, NY: HarperCollins Publishers, Inc., 1973).

5. Burton G. Malkiel, *A Random Walk Down Wall Street* (New York, NY: W. W. Norton & Company, Inc., 1973, 1981, 1985, 1990, 1999, 2003, 2007, 2011, 2012).

6. Peter Lynch and John Rothchild, *Beating the Street* (New York, NY: Simon & Schuster, Inc., 1993).

7. Jesse L. Livermore and Richard Smitten, *How to Trade in Stocks* (New York, NY: McGraw Hill, 1940).

AFTERWORD

1. Sir Arthur Conan Doyle, *The Adventure of the Abbey Grange* (London, UK: The Strand Magazine, 1904).

APPENDIX

1. Risk Tolerance Quiz Source: Grable, J.E. & Lytton, R.H. (1999). Financial risk tolerance revisited: The development of a risk assessment instrument. *Financial Services Review*, 8, 163-181

93175793R00120

Made in the USA
Columbia, SC
06 April 2018